C++ 14 Quick Syntax Reference

Second Edition

Mikael Olsson

Apress®

C++ 14 Quick Syntax Reference

ISBN-13 (pbk): 978-1-4842-1726-9

ISBN-13 (electronic): 978-1-4842-1727-6

Managing Director: Welmoed Spahr
Lead Editor: Steve Anglin
Developmental Editor: Matthew Moodie
Editorial Board: Steve Anglin, Louise Corrigan, Jonathan Gennick, Robert Hutchinson,
    Michelle Lowman, James Markham, Susan McDermott, Matthew Moodie, Jeffrey Pepper,
    Douglas Pundick, Ben Renow-Clarke, Gwenan Spearing
Copy Editor: Karen Jameson
Coordinating Editor: Mark Powers
Compositor: SPi Global
Indexer: SPi Global
Artist: SPi Global

Distributed to the book trade worldwide by Springer Science+Business Media New York, 233 Spring Street, 6th Floor, New York, NY 10013. Phone 1-800-SPRINGER, fax (201) 348-4505, e-mail orders-ny@springer-sbm.com, or visit www.springeronline.com. Apress Media, LLC is a California LLC and the sole member (owner) is Springer Science + Business Media Finance Inc (SSBM Finance Inc). SSBM Finance Inc is a **Delaware** corporation.

For information on translations, please e-mail rights@apress.com, or visit www.apress.com.

Apress and friends of ED books may be purchased in bulk for academic, corporate, or promotional use. eBook versions and licenses are also available for most titles. For more information, reference our Special Bulk Sales–eBook Licensing web page at www.apress.com/bulk-sales.

Any source code or other supplementary material referenced by the author in this text is available to readers at www.apress.com/9781484217269. For detailed information about how to locate your book's source code, go to www.apress.com/source-code/.

Contents at a Glance

Contents

About the Author

Mikael Olsson is a professional web entrepreneur, programmer, and author. He works for an R&D company in Finland where he specializes in software development. In his spare time he writes books and creates websites that summarize various fields of interest. The books he writes are focused on teaching their subject in the most efficient way possible, by explaining only what is relevant and practical without any unnecessary repetition or theory.

Introduction

The C++ programming language is a general purpose multi-paradigm language created by Bjarne Stroustrup. Development of the language started in 1979 under the name "C with classes." As the name implies, it was an extension of the C language with the additional concept of classes. Stroustrup wanted to create a better C that combined the power and efficiency of C with high-level abstractions to better manage large development projects. The resulting language was renamed to C++ (C-Plus-Plus) in 1983. As a deliberate design feature C++ maintains compatibility with C, and so most C code can easily be made to compile in C++.

The introduction of C++ became a major milestone in the software industry as a widely successful language for both system and application development. System programming involves software that controls the computer hardware directly, such as drivers, operating systems, and software for embedded microprocessors. These areas remain the core domain of the language, where resources are scarce and come at a premium. C++ is also widely used for writing applications, which run on top of system software, especially high-performance software such as games, databases, and resource-demanding desktop applications. Despite the introduction of many modern, high-level languages in this domain – such as Java, C#, and Python – C++ still holds its own and overall remains one of the most popular and influential programming languages in use today.

There are several reasons for the widespread adoption of C++. The foremost reason was the rare combination of both high-level and low-level abstractions from the hardware. The low-level efficiency was inherited from C, and the high-level constructs came in part from a simulation language called Simula. This combination makes it possible to write C++ software with the strength of both approaches. Another strong point of the language is that it does not impose a specific programming paradigm on its users. It is designed to give the programmer a lot of freedom by supporting many different programming styles or paradigms, such as procedural, object-oriented, and generic programming.

C++ is updated and maintained by the C++ standards committee. In 1998, the first international standard was published, known informally as C++98. The language has since undergone three more revisions with further extensions, including C++03; C++11; and most recently, C++14, which is the latest ISO standard for the C++ programming language released in 2014.

CHAPTER 1

Hello World

Choosing an IDE

To begin developing in C++ you need a text editor and a C++ compiler. You can get both at the same time by installing an Integrated Development Environment (IDE) that includes support for C++. A good choice is Microsoft's Visual Studio Community Edition, which is a free version of Visual Studio that is available from Microsoft's website.[1] This IDE has built-in support for the C++11 standard and also includes many features of C++14 as of the 2015 version.

Two other popular cross-platform IDEs include NetBeans and Eclipse CDT. Alternatively, you can develop using a simple text editor – such as Notepad – although this is less convenient than using an IDE. If you choose to do so, just create an empty document with a .cpp file extension and open it in the editor of your choice.

Creating a Project

After installing Visual Studio, go ahead and launch the program. You then need to create a project, which will manage the C++ source files and other resources. Go to File ➤ New ➤ Project in Visual Studio to display the New Project window. From there select the Visual C++ template type in the left frame. Then select the Win32 Console Application template in the right frame. At the bottom of the window you can configure the name and location of the project. When you are finished, click the OK button and another dialog box will appear titled Win32 Application Wizard. Click next and a couple of application settings will be displayed. Leave the application type as Console application and check the Empty project checkbox. Then click Finish to let the wizard create your empty project.

Adding a Source File

You have now created a C++ project. In the Solution Explorer pane (View ➤ Solution Explorer) you can see that the project consists of three empty folders: Header Files, Resource Files and Source Files. Right click on the Source Files folder and select Add ➤ New Item. From the Add New Item dialog box choose the C++ File (.cpp) template.

---

[1]`http://www.microsoft.com/visualstudio`

1

Give this source file the name "MyApp" and click the Add button. An empty cpp file will now be added to your project and also opened for you.

Hello World

The first thing to add to the source file is the main function. This is the entry point of the program, and the code inside of the curly brackets is what will be executed when the program runs. The brackets, along with their content, is referred to as a code block, or just a block.

```
int main() {}
```

The first application will simply output the text "Hello World" to the screen. Before this can be done the iostream header needs to be included. This header provides input and output functionality for the program, and is one of the standard library files that come with all C++ compilers. What the #include directive does is effectively to replace the line with everything in the specified header before the file is compiled into an executable.

```
#include <iostream>
int main() {}
```

With iostream included you gain access to several new functions. These are all located in the standard namespace called std, which you can examine by using a double colon, also called the scope resolution operator (::). After typing this in Visual Studio, the IntelliSense window will automatically open, displaying what the namespace contains. Among the members you find the cout stream, which is the standard output stream in C++ that will be used to print text to a console window. It uses two less-than signs known as the insertion operator (<<) to indicate what to output. The string can then be specified, delimited by double quotes, and followed by a semicolon. The semicolon is used in C++ to mark the end of all statements.

```
#include <iostream>

int main()
{
  std::cout << "Hello World";
}
```

Using Namespace

To make things a bit easier you can add a line specifying that the code file uses the standard namespace. You then no longer have to prefix cout with the namespace (std::) since it is now used by default.

```
#include <iostream>
using namespace std;

int main()
{
cout << "Hello World";
}
```

IntelliSense

When writing code in Visual Studio, a window called IntelliSense will pop up wherever there are multiple predetermined alternatives from which to choose. This window can be also brought up manually at any time by pressing Ctrl+Space to provide quick access to any code entities you are able to use within your program. This is a very powerful feature that you should learn to make good use of.

CHAPTER 2

Compile and Run

Visual Studio Compilation

Continuing from the last chapter, the Hello World program is now complete and ready to be compiled and run. You can do this by going to the Debug menu and clicking on Start Without Debugging (Ctrl + F5). Visual Studio then compiles and runs the application which displays the text in a console window.

If you select Start Debugging (F5) from the Debug menu instead, the console window displaying Hello World will close as soon as the main function is finished. To prevent this you can add a call to the cin::get function at the end of main. This function, belonging to the console input stream, will read input from the keyboard until the return key is pressed.

```
#include <iostream>
using namespace std;
int main()
{
  cout << "Hello World";
  cin.get();
}
```

Console Compilation

As an alternative to using an IDE you can also compile source files from a terminal window as long as you have a C++ compiler.[1] For example, on a Linux machine you can use the GNU C++ compiler, which is available on virtually all Unix systems, including Linux and the BSD family, as part of the GNU Compiler Collection (GCC). This compiler can also be installed on Windows by downloading MinGW or on Mac as part of the Xcode development environment.

---

[1]http://www.stroustrup.com/compilers.html

To use the GNU compiler you type its name "g++" in a terminal window and give it the input and output filenames as arguments. It then produces an executable file, which when run gives the same result as one compiled under Windows in Visual Studio.

```
g++ MyApp.cpp -o MyApp.exe
./MyApp.exe
Hello World
```

Comments

Comments are used to insert notes into the source code. They have no effect on the end program and are meant only to enhance the readability of the code, both for you and for other developers. C++ has two kinds of comment notations - single-line and multi-line. The single-line comment starts with // and extends to the end of the line.

```
// single-line comment
```

The multi-line comment may span more than one line and is delimited by /* and */.

```
/* multi-line comment */
```

Keep in mind that whitespace characters – such as comments, spaces, and tabs – are generally ignored by the compiler. This allows you a lot of freedom in how to format your code.

CHAPTER 3

Variables

Variables are used for storing data during program execution.

Data Types

Depending on what data you need to store there are several kinds of built-in data types. These are often called fundamental data types or *primitives*. The integer (whole number) types are short, int, long, and long long. The float, double and long double types are floating-point (real number) types. The char type holds a single character and the bool type contains either a true or false value.

Data Type	Size (byte)	Description
char	1	Integer or character
short	2	
int	4	Integer
long	4 or 8	
long long	8	
float	4	
double	8	Floating-point number
long double	8 or 16	
bool	1	Boolean value

In C++, the exact size and range of data types are not fixed. Instead they are dependent on the system for which the program is compiled. The sizes shown in the table above are those found on most 32-bit systems and are given in C++ bytes. A byte in C++ is the minimum addressable unit of memory, which is guaranteed to be at least 8 bits, but might also be 16 or 32 bits depending on the system. By definition, a char in C++ is 1 byte in size. Furthermore, the int type will have the same size as the processor's word size, so for a 32-bit system the integers will be 32 bits in size. Each integer type in the table must also be at least as large as the one preceding it. The same applies to floating-point types where each one must provide at least as much precision as the preceding one.

7

Declaring Variables

To *declare* (create) a variable you start with the data type you want the variable to hold followed by an *identifier*, which is the name of the variable. The name can consist of letters, numbers and underscores, but it cannot start with a number. It also cannot contain spaces or special characters and must not be a reserved keyword.

```
int myInt;      // correct int _myInt32; // correct
int 32Int;      // incorrect (starts with number)
int Int 32;     // incorrect (contains space)
int Int@32;     // incorrect (contains special character)
int new;        // incorrect (reserved keyword)
```

Assigning Variables

To assign a value to a declared variable the equal sign is used, which is called the assignment operator (=).

```
myInt = 50;
```

The declaration and assignment can be combined into a single statement. When a variable is assigned a value it then becomes *defined*.

```
int myInt = 50;
```

At the same time that the variable is declared there is an alternative way of assigning, or *initializing*, it by enclosing the value in parentheses. This is known as *constructor initialization* and is equivalent to the statement above.

```
int myAlt (50);
```

If you need to create more than one variable of the same type there is a shorthand way of doing it using the comma operator (,).

```
int x = 1, y = 2, z;
```

Once a variable has been defined (declared and assigned), you can use it by simply referencing the variable's name: for example, to print it.

```
std::cout << x << y; // "12"
```

Variable Scope

The scope of a variable refers to the region of code within which it is possible to use that variable. Variables in C++ may be declared both globally and locally. A global variable is declared outside of any code blocks and is accessible from anywhere after it has been declared. A local variable, on the other hand, is declared inside of a function and will only be accessible within that function after it has been declared. The lifetime of a local variable is also limited. A global variable will remain allocated for the duration of the program, while a local variable will be destroyed when its function has finished executing.

```
int globalVar;                // global variable
int main() { int localVar; }  // local variable
```

The default values for these variables are also different. Global variables are automatically initialized to zero by the compiler, whereas local variables are not initialized at all. Uninitialized local variables will therefore contain whatever garbage is already present in that memory location.

```
int globalVar; // initialized to 0

int main()
{
  int localVar; // uninitialized
}
```

Using uninitialized variables is a common programming mistake that can produce unexpected results. It is therefore a good idea to always give your local variables an initial value when they are declared.

```
int main()
{
  int localVar = 0; // initialized to 0
}
```

Integer Types

There are four integer types you can use depending on how large a number you need the variable to hold.

```
char  myChar  = 0; // -128    to +127
short myShort = 0; // -32768 to +32767
int   myInt   = 0; // -2^31   to +2^31-1
long  myLong  = 0; // -2^31   to +2^31-1
```

C++11 standardized a fifth integer type, long long, which is guaranteed to be at least 64-bits large. Many compilers started to support this data type well before the C++11 standard was complete, including the Microsoft C++ compiler.

```
long long myL2 = 0; // -2^63 to +2^63-1
```

To determine the exact size of a data type you can use the sizeof operator. This operator returns the number of bytes that a data type occupies in the system you are compiling for.

```
std::cout << sizeof(myChar)  // 1 byte (per definition)
         << sizeof(myShort) // 2
         << sizeof(myInt)   // 4
         << sizeof(myLong)  // 4
         << sizeof(myL2);   // 8
```

Fixed-sized integer types were added in C++11. These types belong to the std namespace and can be included through the cstdint standard library header.

```
#include <cstdint>
using namespace std;
int8_t  myInt8  = 0; // 8 bits
int16_t myInt16 = 0; // 16 bits
int32_t myInt32 = 0; // 32 bits
int64_t myInt64 = 0; // 64 bits
```

Signed and Unsigned Integers

By default, all the number types in Microsoft C++ are signed and may therefore contain both positive and negative values. To explicitly declare a variable as signed the signed keyword can be used.

```
signed char  myChar  = 0; // -128 to +127
signed short myShort = 0; // -32768 to +32767
signed int   myInt   = 0; // -2^31  to +2^31-1
signed long  myLong  = 0; // -2^31  to +2^31-1
signed long long myL2= 0; // -2^63  to +2^63-1
```

If you only need to store positive values you can declare integer types as unsigned to double their upper range.

```
unsigned char  myChar  = 0; // 0 to 255
unsigned short myShort = 0; // 0 to 65535
unsigned int   myInt   = 0; // 0 to 2^32-1
unsigned long  myLong  = 0; // 0 to 2^32-1
unsigned long long myL2= 0; // 0 to 2^64-1
```

The signed and unsigned keywords may be used as standalone types, which are short for signed int and unsigned int.

```
unsigned uInt; // unsigned int
signed sInt;   // signed int
```

Similarly, the short and long data types are abbreviations of short int and long int.

```
short myShort; // short int
long myLong;   // long int
```

Numeric Literals

In addition to standard decimal notation, integers can also be assigned by using octal or hexadecimal notation. Octal literals use the prefix "0" and hexadecimal literals start with "0x." Both numbers below represent the same number, which in decimal notation is 50.

```
int myOct = 062;  // octal notation (0)
int myHex = 0x32; // hexadecimal notation (0x)
```

As of C++14 there is a binary notation, which uses "0b" as its prefix. This version of the standard also added a digit separator (') which can make it easier to read long numbers. The binary number below represents 50 in decimal notation.

```
int myBin = 0b0011'0010; // binary notation (0b)
```

Floating-Point Types

The floating-point types can store real numbers with different levels of precision.

```
float myFloat;           // ~7 digits
double myDouble;         // ~15 digits
long double myLongDouble; // typically same as double
```

The precision shown above refers to the total number of digits in the number. A float can accurately represent about 7 digits, whereas a double can handle around 15 of them. Trying to assign more than 7 digits to a float means that the least significant digits will get rounded off.

```
myFloat = 12345.678; // rounded to 12345.68
```

Floats and doubles can be assigned by using either decimal or exponential notation. Exponential (scientific) notation is used by adding E or e followed by the decimal exponent.

```
myFloat = 3e2; // 3*10^2 = 300
```

Literal Suffixes

An integer literal (constant) is normally treated as an int by the compiler, or a larger type if needed to fit the value. Suffixes can be added to the literal to change this evaluation. With integers the suffix can be a combination of U and L, for unsigned and long respectively. C++11 also added the LL suffix for the long long type. The order and casing of these letters do not matter.

```
int i = 10;
long l = 10L;
unsigned long ul = 10UL;
```

A floating-point literal is treated as a double unless otherwise specified. The F or f suffix can be used to specify that a literal is of the float type instead. Likewise, the L or l suffix specifies the long double type.

```
float f = 1.23F;
double d = 1.23;
long double ld = 1.23L;
```

The compiler implicitly converts literals to whichever type is necessary, so this type distinction for literals is usually not necessary. If the F suffix is left out when assigning to a float variable, the compiler may give a warning since the conversion from double to float involves a loss of precision.

Char Type

The char type is commonly used to represent ASCII characters. Such character constants are enclosed in single quotes and can be stored in a variable of char type.

```
char c = 'x'; // assigns 120 (ASCII for 'x')
```

The conversion between the number stored in the char and the character shown when the char is printed occurs automatically.

```
std::cout << c; // prints 'x'
```

For another integer type to be displayed as a character it has to be explicitly cast to char. An explicit cast is performed by placing the desired data type in parentheses before the variable or constant that is to be converted.

```
int i = c;              // assigns 120
std::cout << i;         // prints 120
std::cout << (char)i; // prints 'x'
```

Bool Type

The bool type can store a Boolean value, which is a value that can only be either true or false. These values are specified with the true and false keywords.

```
bool b = false; // true or false value
```

CHAPTER 4

Operators

A numerical operator is a symbol that makes the program perform a specific mathematical or logical manipulation. The numerical operators in C++ can be grouped into five types: arithmetic, assignment, comparison, logical and bitwise operators.

Arithmetic Operators

There are the four basic arithmetic operators, as well as the modulus operator (%) which is used to obtain the division remainder.

```
int x = 3 + 2; // 5 // addition
    x = 3 - 2; // 1 // subtraction
    x = 3 * 2; // 6 // multiplication
    x = 3 / 2; // 1 // division
    x = 3 % 2; // 1 // modulus (division remainder)
```

Notice that the division sign gives an incorrect result. This is because it operates on two integer values and will therefore truncate the result and return an integer. To get the correct value, one of the numbers must be explicitly converted to a floating-point number.

```
float f = 3 / (float)2; // 1.5
```

Assignment Operators

The second group is the assignment operators. Most importantly, the assignment operator (=) itself, which assigns a value to a variable.

Combined Assignment Operators

A common use of the assignment and arithmetic operators is to operate on a variable and then to save the result back into that same variable. These operations can be shortened with the combined assignment operators.

```
x += 5; // x = x+5;
x -= 5; // x = x-5;
x *= 5; // x = x*5;
x /= 5; // x = x/5;
x %= 5; // x = x%5;
```

Increment and Decrement Operators

Another common operation is to increment or decrement a variable by one. This can be simplified with the increment (++) and decrement (--) operators.

```
x++; // x = x+1;
x--; // x = x-1;
```

Both of these can be used either before or after a variable.

```
x++; // post-increment
x--; // post-decrement
++x; // pre-increment
--x; // pre-decrement
```

The result on the variable is the same whichever is used. The difference is that the post-operator returns the original value before it changes the variable, while the pre-operator changes the variable first and then returns the value.

```
int x, y;
x = 5; y = x++; // y=5, x=6
x = 5; y = ++x; // y=6, x=6
```

Comparison Operators

The comparison operators compare two values and return either true or false. They are mainly used to specify conditions, which are expressions that evaluate to either true or false.

```
bool b = (2 == 3); // false // equal to
     b = (2 != 3); // true  // not equal to
     b = (2 > 3);  // false // greater than
     b = (2 < 3);  // true  // less than
     b = (2 >= 3); // false // greater than or equal to
     b = (2 <= 3); // true  // less than or equal to
```

Logical Operators

The logical operators are often used together with the comparison operators. Logical and (&&) evaluates to true if both the left and right sides are true, and logical or (| |) is true if either the left or right side is true. For inverting a Boolean result there is the logical not (!) operator. Note that for both "logical and" and "logical or" the right-hand side will not be evaluated if the result is already determined by the left-hand side.

```
bool b = (true && false); // false // logical and
     b = (true || false); // true  // logical or
     b = !(true);         // false // logical not
```

Bitwise Operators

The bitwise operators can manipulate individual bits inside an integer. For example, the "bitwise or" operator (|) makes the resulting bit 1 if the bits are set on either side of the operator.

```
int x = 5 & 4;  // 101 & 100 = 100 (4)  // and
x = 5 | 4;      // 101 | 100 = 101 (5)  // or
x = 5 ^ 4;      // 101 ^ 100 = 001 (1)  // xor
x = 4 << 1;     // 100 << 1 =1000 (8)  // left shift
x = 4 >> 1;     // 100 >> 1 =  10 (2)  // right shift
x = ~4;         // ~00000100 = 11111011 (-5) // invert
```

The bitwise operators also have combined assignment operators.

```
int x=5; x &= 4; // 101 & 100 = 100 (4) // and
    x=5; x |= 4; // 101 | 100 = 101 (5) // or
    x=5; x ^= 4; // 101 ^ 100 = 001 (1) // xor
    x=5; x <<= 1;// 101 << 1 =1010 (10)// left shift
    x=5; x >>= 1;// 101 >> 1 =  10 (2) // right shift
```

Operator Precedence

In C++, expressions are normally evaluated from left to right. However, when an expression contains multiple operators, the precedence of those operators decides the order in which they are evaluated. The order of precedence can be seen in the following table, where the operator with the lowest precedence will be evaluated first. This same basic order also applies to many other languages, such as C, Java, and C#.

Pre	Operator	Pre	Operator
1	::	9	== !=
2	() [] . -> x++ x--	10	&
3	! ~ ++x --x x* x& (type)	11	^
4	.* ->*	12	|
5	* / %	13	&&
6	+ -	14	||
7	<< >>	15	?: = op=
8	< <= > >=	16	,

To give an example, logical and (&&) binds weaker than relational operators, which in turn bind weaker than arithmetic operators.

```
bool b = 2+3 > 1*4 && 5/5 == 1; // true
```

To make things clearer, parentheses can be used to specify which part of the expression will be evaluated first. As seen in the table, parentheses are among the operators with lowest precedence.

```
bool b = ((2+3) > (1*4)) && ((5/5) == 1); // true
```

CHAPTER 5

Pointers

A pointer is a variable that contains the memory address of another variable, called the *pointee*.

Creating Pointers

Pointers are declared as any other variable, except that an asterisk (*) is placed between the data type and the pointer's name. The data type used determines what type of memory it will point to.

```
int* p; // pointer to an integer
int *q; // alternative syntax
```

A pointer can point to a variable of the same type by prefixing that variable with an ampersand, in order to retrieve its address and assign it to the pointer. The ampersand is known as the address-of operator (&).

```
int i = 10;
p = &i; // address of i assigned to p
```

Dereferencing Pointers

The pointer above now contains the memory address to the integer variable. Referencing the pointer will retrieve this address. To obtain the actual value stored in that address the pointer must be prefixed with an asterisk, known as the dereference operator (*).

```
std::cout << "Address of i: " <<  p; // ex. 0017FF1C
std::cout << "Value of i: "   << *p; // 10
```

When writing to the pointer, the same method is used. Without the asterisk the pointer is assigned a new memory address, and with the asterisk the actual value of the variable pointed to will be updated.

```
p = &i;  // address of i assigned to p
*p = 20; // value of i changed through p
```

If a second pointer is created and assigned the value of the first pointer it will then get a copy of the first pointer's memory address.

```
int* p2 = p; // copy of p (copies address stored in p)
```

Pointing to a Pointer

Sometimes it can be useful to have a pointer that can point to another pointer. This is done by declaring a pointer with two asterisks and then assigning it the address of the pointer that it will reference. This way when the address stored in the first pointer changes, the second pointer can follow that change.

```
int** r = &p; // pointer to p (assigns address of p)
```

Referencing the second pointer now gives the address of the first pointer. Dereferencing the second pointer gives the address of the variable and dereferencing it again gives the value of the variable.

```
std::cout << "Address of p: " << r;   // ex. 0017FF28 std::cout << "Address
of i: " << *r;  // ex. 0017FF1C std::cout << "Value of i: "   << **r; // 20
```

Dynamic Allocation

One of the main usages of pointers is to allocate memory during run-time – so called *dynamic allocation*. In the examples so far, the programs have only had as much memory available as has been declared for the variables at compile-time. This is referred to as *static allocation*. If any additional memory is needed at run-time, the new operator has to be used. This operator allows for dynamic allocation of memory, which can only be accessed through pointers. The new operator takes either a primitive data type or an object as its argument, and it will return a pointer to the allocated memory.

```
int* d = new int; // dynamic allocation
```

An important thing to know about dynamic allocation is that the allocated memory will not be released like the rest of the program memory when it is no longer required. Instead, it has to be manually released with the delete keyword. This allows you to control the lifetime of a dynamically allocated object, but it also means that you are responsible for deleting it once it is no longer needed. Forgetting to delete memory that has been allocated with the new keyword will give the program memory leaks, because that memory will stay allocated until the program shuts down.

```
delete d; // release allocated memory
```

Null Pointer

A pointer should be set to zero when it is not assigned to a valid address. Such a pointer is called a *null pointer*. Doing this will allow you to check whether the pointer can be safely dereferenced, because a valid pointer will never be zero.

For example, although the previous pointer has had its memory released, its stored address still points to a now inaccessible memory location. Trying to dereference such a pointer will cause a run-time error. To help prevent this, the deleted pointer should be set to zero. Note that trying to delete an already deleted null pointer is safe. However, if the pointer has not been set to zero, attempting to delete it again will cause memory corruption and possibly crash the program.

```
delete d;
d = 0; // mark as null pointer
delete d; // safe
```

Since you may not always know whether a pointer is valid, a check should be made whenever a pointer is dereferenced to make sure that it is not zero.

```
if (d != 0) { *d = 10; } // check for null pointer
```

The constant NULL can also be used to signify a null pointer. NULL is typically defined as zero in C++, making the choice of which to use a matter of preference. The constant is defined in the stdio.h standard library file, which is included through iostream.

```
#include <iostream>
// ...
if (d != NULL) { *d = 10; } // check for null pointer
```

C++11 introduced the keyword nullptr to distinguish between 0 and a null pointer. The advantage of using nullptr is that unlike NULL, it will not implicitly convert to an integer type. The literal has its own type, nullptr_t, which can only be implicitly converted to pointer and bool types.

```
int* p = nullptr; // ok
int  i = nullptr; // error
bool b = nullptr; // ok (false)

nullptr_t mynull = nullptr; // ok
```

CHAPTER 6

References

References allow a programmer to create a new name for a variable. They provide a simpler, safer and less powerful alternative to pointers.

Creating References

A reference is declared in the same way as a regular variable, except that an ampersand is appended between the data type and the variable name. Furthermore, at the same time as the reference is declared it must be initialized with a variable of the specified type.

```
int x = 5;
int& r = x; // r is an alias to x
int &s = x; // alternative syntax
```

Once the reference has been assigned, or seated, it can never be reseated to another variable. The reference has in effect become an alias for the variable and can be used exactly as though it was the original variable.

```
r = 10; // assigns value to r/x
```

References and Pointers

A reference is similar to a pointer that always points to the same thing. However, while a pointer is a variable that points to another variable, a reference is only an alias and does not have an address of its own.

```
int* ptr = &x; // ptr assigned address to x
```

Reference and Pointer Guideline

Generally, whenever a pointer does not need to be reassigned a reference should be used instead, because a reference is safer than a pointer since it must always refer to a variable. This means that there is no need to check if a reference refers to null, as should be done with pointers. It is possible for a reference to be invalid – for example when a reference refers to a null pointer – but it is much easier to avoid this kind of mistake with references than it is with pointers.

```
int* ptr = 0; // null pointer
int& ref = *ptr;
ref = 10;      // segmentation fault (invalid memory access)
```

Rvalue Reference

With C++11 came a new kind of reference called an rvalue reference. This reference can bind and modify temporary objects (rvalues), such as literal values and function return values. An rvalue reference is formed by placing two ampersands after the type.

```
int&& ref = 1 + 2; // rvalue reference
```

The rvalue reference extends the lifetime of the temporary object and allows it to be used like an ordinary variable.

```
ref += 3;
cout << ref; // "6"
```

The benefit of rvalue references is that they allow unnecessary copying to be avoided when dealing with temporary objects. This offers greater performance, particularly when handling larger types, such as strings and objects.

CHAPTER 7

Arrays

An array is a data structure used for storing a collection of values that all have the same data type.

Array Declaration and Allocation

To declare an array you start as you would a normal variable declaration, but in addition append a set of square brackets following the array's name. The brackets contain the number of elements in the array. The default values for these elements are the same as for variables – elements in global arrays are initialized to their default values and elements in local arrays remain uninitialized.

```
int myArray[3]; // integer array with 3 elements
```

Array Assignment

To assign values to the elements you can reference them one at a time by placing the element's index inside the square brackets, starting with zero.

```
myArray[0] = 1;
myArray[1] = 2;
myArray[2] = 3;
```

Alternatively, you can assign values at the same time as the array is declared by enclosing them in curly brackets. The specified array length may optionally be left out to let the array size be decided by the number of values assigned.

```
int myArray[3] = { 1, 2, 3 };
int myArray[] = { 1, 2, 3 };
```

Once the array elements are initialized they can be accessed by referencing the index of the element you want.

```
std::cout << myArray[0]; // 1
```

Multi-dimensional Arrays

Arrays can be made multi-dimensional by adding more sets of square brackets. As with single-dimensional arrays, they can either be filled in one at a time or all at once during the declaration.

```
int myArray[2][2] = { { 0, 1 }, { 2, 3 } };
myArray[0][0] = 0;
myArray[0][1] = 1;
```

The extra curly brackets are optional, but including them is good practice since it makes the code easier to understand.

```
int mArray[2][2] = { 0, 1, 2, 3 }; // alternative
```

Dynamic Arrays

Because the arrays above are made up of static (non-dynamic) memory, their size must be determined before execution. Therefore, the size needs to be a constant value. In order to create an array with a size that is not known until run-time you need to use dynamic memory, which is allocated with the new keyword and must be assigned to a pointer or reference.

```
int* p = new int[3]; // dynamically allocated array
```

An array in C++ behaves as a constant pointer to the first element in the array. The referencing of array elements can therefore be made just as well with pointer arithmetic. By incrementing the pointer by one you move to the next element in the array, because changes to a pointer's address are implicitly multiplied by the size of the pointer's data type.

```
*(p+1) = 10; // p[1] = 10;
```

Array Size

Just as with any other pointer, it is possible to exceed the valid range of an array and thereby rewrite some adjacent memory. This should always be avoided since it can lead to unexpected results or crash the program.

```
int myArray[2] = { 1, 2 };
myArray[2] = 3; // out of bounds error
```

To determine the length of a regular (statically allocated) array, the sizeof operator can be used.

```
int length = sizeof(myArray) / sizeof(int); // 2
```

This method cannot be used for dynamically allocated arrays. The only way to determine the size of such an array is through the variable used in its allocation.

```
int size = 3;
int* p = new int[size]; // dynamically allocated array
```

When you are done using a dynamic array you must remember to delete it. This is done using the delete keyword with an appended set of square brackets.

```
delete[] p; // release allocated array
```

CHAPTER 8

String

The stringclass in C++ is used to store string values. Before a string can be declared the string header must first be included. The standard namespace can also be included since the string class is part of that namespace.

```
#include <string>
using namespace std;
```

Strings can then be declared like any other data type. To assign a string value to a string variable, delimit the literals by double quotes and assign them to the variable. The initial value can also be assigned through constructor initialization at the same time as the string is declared.

```
string h = "Hello";
string w (" World");
```

String Combining

The plus sign, known as the concatenation operator (+) in this context, is used to combine two strings. It has an accompanying assignment operator (+=) to append a string.

```
string a = h + w; // Hello World
h += w;           // Hello World
```

The concatenation operator will work as long as one of the strings it operates on is a C++ string.

```
string b = "Hello" + w; // ok
```

It is not able to concatenate two C strings or two string literals. To do this, one of the values has to be explicitly cast to a string.

```
char *c = "World";            // C-style string
b = (string)c + c;            // ok
b = "Hello" + (string)" World"; // ok
```

String literals will also be implicitly combined if the plus sign is left out.

```
b = "Hel" "lo"; // ok
```

Escape Characters

A string literal can be extended to more than one line by putting a backslash sign (\) at the end of each line.

```
string s = "Hello \ World";
```

To add a new line to the string itself, the escape character "\n" is used.

```
s = "Hello \n World";
```

This backslash notation is used to write special characters, such as tab or form feed characters.

Character	Meaning	Character	Meaning
\n	newline	\f	form feed
\t	horizontal tab	\a	alert sound
\v	vertical tab	\'	single quote
\b	Backspace	\"	double quote
\r	carriage return	\\	backslash
\0	null character		

Additionally, any one of the 128 ASCII characters can be expressed by writing a backslash followed by the ASCII code for that character, represented as either an octal or hexadecimal number.

```
"\07F"  // octal character (0-07F)
"\0x177" // hexadecimal character (0-0x177)
```

As of C++11, escape characters can be ignored by adding a "R" before the string along with a set of parentheses within the double quotes. This is called a raw string and can be used, for instance, to make file paths more readable.

```
string escaped = "c:\\Windows\\System32\\cmd.exe";
string raw = R"(c:\Windows\System32\cmd.exe)";
```

String Compare

The way to compare two strings is simply by using the equal to operator (==). This will not compare the memory addresses of the strings, as is the case of C strings.

```
string s = "Hello";
bool b = (s == "Hello"); // true
```

String Functions

The string class has a lot of functions. Among the most useful ones are the length and size functions, which both return the number of characters in the string. Their return type is size_t, which is an unsigned data type used to hold the size of an object. This is simply an alias for one of the built-in data types, but which one it is defined as varies between compilers. The alias is defined in the crtdefs.h standard library file, which is included through iostream.

```
size_t i = s.length(); // 5, length of string
i = s.size();          // 5, same as length()
```

Another useful function is substr (substring), which requires two parameters. The second parameter is the number of characters to return starting from the position specified in the first parameter.

```
s.substr(0,2); // "He"
```

A single character can also be extracted or changed by using the array notation.

```
char c = s[0]; // 'H'
```

String Encodings

A string enclosed within double quotes produces an array of the char type, which can only hold 256 unique symbols. To support larger character sets the wide character type wchar_t is provided. String literals of this type are created by prepending the string with a capital "L". The resulting array can be stored using the wstring class. This class works like the basic string class but uses the wchar_t character type instead.

```
wstring s1 = L"Hello";
wchar_t *s2 = L"Hello";
```

Fixed-size character types were introduced in C++11, namely char16_t and char32_t. These types provide definite representations of the UTF-16 and UTF-32 encodings respectively. UTF-16 string literals are prefixed with "u" and can be stored using the u16string class. Likewise, UTF-32 string literals are prefixed with "U" and are stored in the u32string class. The prefix "u8" was also added to represent a UTF-8 encoded string literal.

```
string s3 = u8"UTF-8 string";
u16string s4 = u"UTF-16 string";
u32string s5 = U"UTF-32 string";
```

Specific Unicode characters can be inserted into a string literal using the escape character "\u" followed by a hexadecimal number representing the character.

```
string s6 = u8"An asterisk: \u002A";
```

CHAPTER 9

Conditionals

Conditional statements are used to execute different code blocks based on different conditions.

If Statement

The if statement will only execute if the expression inside the parentheses is evaluated to true. In C++, this does not have to be a Boolean expression. It can be any expression that evaluates to a number, in which case zero is false and all other numbers are true.

```
if (x < 1) {
    cout << x << " < 1";
}
```

To test for other conditions, the if statement can be extended by any number of else if clauses.

```
else if (x > 1) {
    cout << x << " > 1";
}
```

The if statement can have one else clause at the end, which will execute if all previous conditions are false.

```
else {
    cout << x << " == 1";
}
```

As for the curly brackets, they can be left out if only a single statement needs to be executed conditionally. However, it is considered good practice to always include them since they improve readability.

```
if (x < 1)
    cout << x << " < 1";
else if (x > 1)
    cout << x << " > 1";
else
    cout << x << " == 1";
```

Switch Statement

The switch statement checks for equality between an integer and a series of case labels, and then passes execution to the matching case. It may contain any number of case clauses and it can end with a default label for handling all other cases.

```
switch (x)
{
    case 0: cout << x << " is 0"; break;
    case 1: cout << x << " is 1"; break;
    default: cout << x << " is not 1 or 2"; break;
}
```

Note that the statements after each case label end with the break keyword to skip the rest of the switch. If the break is left out, execution will fall through to the next case, which can be useful if several cases need to be evaluated in the same way.

Ternary Operator

In addition to the if and switch statements there is the ternary operator (?:) that can replace a single if/else clause. This operator takes three expressions. If the first one is true then the second expression is evaluated and returned, and if it is false, the third one is evaluated and returned.

```
x = (x < 0.5) ? 0 : 1; // ternary operator (?:)
```

C++ allows expressions to be used as stand-alone code statements. Because of this the ternary operator cannot just be used as an expression, but also as a statement.

```
(x < 0.5) ? x = 0 : x = 1; // alternative syntax
```

The programming term *expression* refers to code that evaluates to a value, whereas a *statement* is a code segment that ends with a semicolon or a closing curly bracket.

CHAPTER 10

Loops

There are three looping structures available in C++, all of which are used to execute a specific code block multiple times. Just as with the conditional if statement, the curly brackets for the loops can be left out if there is only one statement in the code block.

While Loop

The while loop runs through the code block only if its condition is true, and will continue looping for as long as the condition remains true. Bear in mind that the condition is only checked at the start of each iteration (loop).

```
int i = 0;
while (i < 10) { cout << i++; } // 0-9
```

Do-while Loop

The do-while loop works in the same way as the while loop, except that it checks the condition after the code block. It will therefore always run through the code block at least once. Notice that this loop ends with a semicolon.

```
int j = 0;
do { cout << j++; } while (j < 10); // 0-9
```

For Loop

The for loop is used to run through a code block a specific number of times. It uses three parameters. The first one initializes a counter and is always executed once before the loop. The second parameter holds the condition for the loop and is checked before each iteration. The third parameter contains the increment of the counter and is executed at the end of each loop.

```
for (int k = 0; k < 10; k++) { cout << k; } // 0-9
```

The for loop has several variations. For starters, the first and third parameters can be split into several statements by using the comma operator.

```
for (int k = 0, m = 0; k < 10; k++, m--) {
    cout << k+m; // 0x10
}
```

There is also the option of leaving out any one of the parameters.

```
for (;;) {
    cout << "infinite loop";
}
```

C++11 introduced a range-based for loop syntax for iterating through arrays and other container types. At each iteration the next element in the array is bound to the reference variable, and the loop continues until it has gone through the entire array.

```
int a[3] = {1, 2, 3};
for (int &i : a) {
    cout <<i; // "123"
}
```

Break and Continue

There are two jump statements that can be used inside loops: break and continue. The break keyword ends the loop structure, and continue skips the rest of the current iteration and continues at the beginning of the next iteration.

```
for (int i = 0; i < 10; i++)
{
    break;    // end loop
    continue; // start next iteration
}
```

Goto Statement

A third jump statement that may be useful to know of is goto, which performs an unconditional jump to a specified label. This instruction is generally never used since it tends to make the flow of execution difficult to follow.

```
goto myLabel; // jump to label
myLabel:      // label declaration
```

CHAPTER 11

Functions

Functions are reusable code blocks that will only execute when called.

Defining Functions

A function can be created by typing void followed by the function's name, a set of parentheses and a code block. The void keyword means that the function will not return a value. The naming convention for functions is the same as for variables – a descriptive name with each word initially capitalized, except for the first one.

```
void myFunction()
{
  cout << "Hello World";
}
```

Calling Functions

The function above will simply print out a text message when it is called. To invoke it from the main function the function's name is specified followed by a set of parentheses.

```
int main()
{
  myFunction(); // "Hello World"
}
```

Function Parameters

The parentheses that follow the function name are used to pass arguments to the function. To do this the corresponding parameters must first be added to the function declaration in the form of a comma separated list.

```
void myFunction(string a, string b)
{
  cout << a + " " + b;
}
```

A function can be defined to take any number of parameters, and they can have any data types. Just ensure the function is called with the same types and number of arguments.

```
myFunction("Hello", "World"); // "Hello World"
```

To be precise, *parameters* appear in function definitions, while *arguments* appear in function calls. However, the two terms are sometimes used interchangeably.

Default Parameter Values

It is possible to specify default values for parameters by assigning them a value inside the parameter list.

```
void myFunction(string a, string b = "Earth")
{
  cout << a + " " + b;
}
```

Then, if that argument is unspecified when the function is called the default value will be used instead. For this to work it is important that the parameters with default values are to the right of those without default values.

```
myFunction("Hello"); // "Hello Earth"
```

Function Overloading

A function in C++ can be defined multiple times with different arguments. This is a powerful feature called function overloading that allows a function to handle a variety of parameters without the programmer using the function needing to be aware of it.

```
void myFunction(string a, string b) { cout << a+" "+b; }
void myFunction(string a)           { cout << a; }
void myFunction(int a)              { cout << a; }
```

Return Statement

A function can return a value. The void keyword is then replaced with the data type the function will return, and the return keyword is added to the function's body followed by an argument of the specified return type.

```
int getSum(int a, int b)
{
    return a + b;
}
```

Return is a jump statement that causes the function to exit and return the specified value to the place where the function was called. For example, the function above can be passed as an argument to the output stream since the function evaluates to an integer.

```
cout << getSum(5, 10); // 15
```

The return statement can also be used in void functions to exit before the end block is reached.

```
void dummy() { return; }
```

Note that although the main function is set to return an integer type, it does not have to explicitly return a value. This is because the compiler will automatically add a return zero statement to the end of the main function.

```
int main() { return 0; }
```

Forward Declaration

An important thing to keep in mind in C++ is that functions must be declared before they can be called. This does not mean that the function has to be implemented before it is called. It only means that the function's header needs to be specified at the beginning of the source file, so that the compiler knows that the function exists. This kind of forward declaration is known as a *prototype*.

```
void myFunction(int a); // prototype
int main()
{
  myFunction(0);
}
void myFunction(int a) {}
```

The parameter names in the prototype do not need to be included. Only the data types must be specified.

```
void myFunction(int);
```

39

Pass by Value

In C++, variables of both primitive and object data types are by default passed by value. This means that only a copy of the value or object is passed to the function. Therefore, changing the parameter in any way will not affect the original, and passing a large object will be very slow.

```cpp
#include <iostream>
#include <string>
using namespace std;

void change(int i) { i = 10; }
void change(string s) { s = "Hello World"; }

int main()
{
  int x = 0;     // value type change(x);     // value is passed
  cout << x;     // 0

  string y = ""; // reference type
  change(y);     // object copy is passed
  cout << y;     // ""
}
```

Pass by Reference

Alternatively, to instead pass a variable by reference you just need to add an ampersand before the parameter's name in the function's definition. When arguments are passed by reference, both primitive and object data types can be changed or replaced and the changes will affect the original.

```cpp
void change(int& i) { i = 10; }

int main()
{
  int x = 0; // value type
  change(x); // reference is passed
  cout << x; // 10
}
```

Pass by Address

As an alternative to passing by reference, arguments may also be passed by address using pointers. This passing technique serves the same purpose as passing by reference, but uses pointer syntax instead.

```
void change(int* i) { *i = 10; }

int main()
{
  int x = 0;   // value type
  change(&x); // address is passed
  cout << x;   // 10
}
```

Return by Value, Reference or Address

In addition to passing variables by value, reference or address, a variable may also be returned in one of these ways. Most commonly, a function returns by value, in which case a copy of the value is returned to the caller.

```
int byVal(int i) { return i + 1; }

int main()
{
  int a = 10;
  cout << byVal(a); // 11
}
```

To return by reference instead, an ampersand is placed after the function's return type. The function must then return a variable and may not return an expression or literal, as can be done when using return by value. The variable returned should never be a local variable, since the memory to these variables is released when the function ends. Instead, return by reference is commonly used to return an argument that has also been passed to the function by reference.

```
int& byRef(int& i) { return i; }

int main()
{
  int a = 10;
  cout << byRef(a); // 10
}
```

To return by address the dereference operator is appended to the function's return type. This return technique has the same two restrictions as when returning by reference – the address of a variable must be returned and that returned variable must not be local to the function.

```
int* byAdr(int* i) { return i; }

int main()
{
   int a = 10;
   cout << *byAdr(&a); // 10
}
```

Inline Functions

A thing to keep in mind when using functions is that every time a function is called, a performance overhead occurs. To potentially remove this overhead you can recommend that the compiler inlines the calls to a specific function by using the inline function modifier. This keyword is best suited for small functions that are called inside loops. It should not be used on larger functions since inlining these can severely increase the size of the code, which will instead decrease performance.

```
inline int myInc(int i) { return i++; }
```

Note that the inline keyword is only a recommendation. The compiler may in its attempts to optimize the code choose to ignore this recommendation and it may also inline functions that do not have the inline modifier.

Auto and Decltype

Two new keywords were introduced in C++11: auto and decltype. Both of these keywords are used for type deduction during compilation. The auto keyword works as a placeholder for a type and instructs the compiler to automatically deduce the type of the variable based on its initializer.

```
auto i = 5;      // int
auto d = 3.14;   // double
auto b = false;  // bool
```

Auto translates to the core type of the initializer, which means that any reference and constant specifiers are dropped.

```
int& iRef = i;
auto myAuto = iRef; // int
```

Dropped specifiers can be manually reapplied as needed. The ampersand here creates a regular (lvalue) reference.

```
auto& myRef = iRef; // int&
```

Alternatively, two ampersands can be used. This normally designates an rvalue reference, but in the case of auto it makes the compiler automatically deduce either an rvalue or an lvalue reference, based on the given initializer.

```
int i = 1;
auto&& a = i; // int& (lvalue reference)
auto&& b = 2; // int&& (rvalue reference)
```

The auto specifier may be used anywhere a variable is declared and initialized. For instance, the type of the for loop iterator below is set to auto, since the compiler can easily deduce the type.

```
#include <vector>
using namespace std;
// ...
vector<int> myVector { 1, 2, 3 };
for (auto& x : myVector) { cout << x; } // "123"
```

Prior to C++11 there was no range-based for loop or auto specifier. Iterating over a vector then required a more verbose syntax.

```
for(vector<int>::size_type i = 0; i != myVector.size(); i++) {
    cout << myVector[i]; // "123"
}
```

The decltype specifier works similar to auto, except it deduces the exact declared type of a given expression, including references. This expression is specified in parentheses.

```
decltype(3) b = 3; // int&&
```

In C++14, auto may be used as the expression for decltype. The keyword auto is then replaced with the initializing expression, allowing the exact type of the initializer to be deduced.

```
decltype(auto) = 3; // int&&
```

Using auto is often the simpler choice when an initializer is available. Decltype is mainly used to forward function return types, without having to consider whether it is a reference or value type.

```
decltype(5) getFive() { return 5; } // int
```

C++11 added a trailing return type syntax, which allows a function's return value to be specified after the parameter list, following the arrow operator (->). This enables the parameter to be used when deducing the return type with decltype. The use of auto in this context in C++11 just means that trailing return type syntax is being used.

```
auto getValue(int x) -> decltype(x) { return x; } // int
```

The ability to use auto for return type deduction was added in C++14. This enabled the core return type to be deduced directly from the return statement,

```
auto getValue(int x) { return x; } // int
```

Moreover, auto can be used together with decltype to deduce the exact type following the rules of decltype.

```
decltype(auto) getRef(int& x) { return x; } // int&
```

The main use for type deduction is to reduce the verbosity of the code and improve readability, particularly when declaring complicated types where the type is either difficult to know or difficult to write. Keep in mind that in modern IDEs you can hover over a variable to check its type, even if the type has been automatically deduced.

Lambda Functions

C++11 adds the ability to create lambda functions, which are unnamed function objects. This provides a compact way to define functions at their point of use, without having to create a named function somewhere else. The following example creates a lambda that accepts two int arguments and returns their sum.

```
auto sum = [](int x, int y) -> int
{
  return x + y;
};
```

```
cout << sum(2, 3); // "5"
```

Including the return type is optional if the compiler can deduce the return value from the lambda. In C++11 this required the lambda to contain just a single return statement, whereas C++14 extended return type deduction to any lambda function. Note that the arrow operator (->) is also omitted when leaving out the return type.

```
auto sum = [](int x, int y) { return x + y; };
```

C++11 requires lambda parameters to be declared with concrete types. This requirement was relaxed in C++14, allowing lambdas to use auto type deduction.

```
auto sum = [](auto x, auto y) { return x + y; };
```

Lambdas are typically used for specifying simple functions that are only referenced once, often by passing the function object as an argument to another function. This can be done using a function wrapper with a matching parameter list and return type, as in the following example.

```cpp
#include <iostream>
#include <functional>
using namespace std;

void call(int arg, function<void(int)> func) {
  func(arg);
}

int main() {
 auto printSquare = [](int x) { cout << x*x; };
 call(2, printSquare); // "4"
}
```

All lambdas start with a set of square brackets, called the capture clause. This clause specifies variables from the surrounding scope that can be used within the lambda body. This effectively passes additional arguments to the lambda, without the need to specify these in the parameter list of the function wrapper. The previous example can therefore be rewritten in the following way.

```cpp
void call(function<void()> func) { func(); }

int main() {
 int i = 2;
 auto printSquare = [i]() { cout << i*i; };
 call(printSquare); // "4"
}
```

The variable is here captured by value and so a copy is used within the lambda. Variables can also be captured by reference using the familiar ampersand prefix. Note that the lambda is here defined and called in the same statement.

```cpp
int a = 1;
[&a](int x) { a += x; }(2);
cout << a; // "3"
```

It is possible to specify a default capture mode, to indicate how any unspecified variable used inside the lambda is to be captured. A [=] means the variables are captured by value and [&] captures them by reference. Variables captured by value are normally constant, but the mutable specifier can be used to allow such variables to be modified.

```cpp
int a = 1, b = 1;
[&, b]() mutable { b++; a += b; }();
cout << a << b; // "31"
```

As of C++14, variables may also be initialized inside the capture clause. If there is no variable with the same name in the outer scope, the variable's type will be deduced as if by auto.

```
int a = 1;
[&, b = 2]() { a += b; }();
cout << a; // "3"
```

CHAPTER 12

Class

A class is a template used to create objects. To define one the `class` keyword is used followed by a name, a code block and a semicolon. The naming convention for classes is mixed case, meaning that each word should be initially capitalized.

```
class MyRectangle {};
```

Class members can be declared inside the class; the two main kinds are fields and methods. Fields are variables and they hold the state of the object. Methods are functions and they define what the object can do.

```
class MyRectangle
{
    int x, y;
};
```

Class Methods

A method belonging to a class is normally declared as a prototype inside of the class, and the actual implementation is placed after the class's definition. The method's name outside the class then needs to be prefixed with the class name and the scope resolution operator in order to designate to which class the method definition belongs.

```
class MyRectangle
{
    int x, y;
    int getArea();
};

int MyRectangle::getArea() { return x * y; }
```

Inline Methods

If the method is short and you want to recommend to the compiler that the function's code should be inserted (inlined) into the caller's code, one way to do this would be to use the `inline` keyword in the method's definition.

```
inline int MyRectangle::getArea() { return x * y; }
```

A more convenient way is to simply define the method inside of the class. This will implicitly recommend to the compiler that the method should be inlined.

```
class MyRectangle
{
    int x, y;
    int getArea() { return x * y; }
};
```

Object Creation

The class definition is now complete. In order to use it you first have to create an object of the class, also called an instance. This can be done in the same way as variables are declared.

```
int main()
{
    MyRectangle r; // object creation
}
```

Accessing Object Members

Before the members that this object contains can be accessed, they first need to be declared as public in the class definition, by using the `public` keyword followed by a colon.

```
class MyRectangle
{
public:
    int x, y;
    int getArea() { return x * y; }
};
```

The members of this object can now be reached using the dot operator (`.`) after the instance name.

```
r.x = 10;
r.y = 5;
int z = r.getArea(); // 50 (5*10)
```

Any number of objects can be created based on a class, and each one of them will have its own set of fields and methods.

```
MyRectangle r2; // another instance of MyRectangle
r2.x = 25;      // not same as r.x
```

When using an object pointer, the arrow operator (->) allows access to the object's members. This operator behaves like the dot operator, except that it dereferences the pointer first. It is used exclusively with pointers to objects.

```
MyRectangle r;
MyRectangle *p = &r; // object pointer

p->getArea();
(*p).getArea();      // alternative syntax
```

Forward Declaration

Classes, just like functions, must be declared before they can be referenced. If a class definition does not appear before the first reference to that class, a class prototype can be specified above the reference instead.

```
class MyClass; // class prototype
```

This forward declaration allows the class to be referenced in any context that does not require the class to be fully defined.

```
class MyClass; // class prototype
MyClass* p; // allowed
MyClass f(MyClass&); // allowed

MyClass o; // error, definition required
sizeof(MyClass); // error, definition required
```

Note that even with a prototype, you still cannot create an object of a class before it has been defined.

CHAPTER 13

Constructor

In addition to fields and methods, a class can contain a *constructor*. This is a special kind of method used to construct, or *instantiate*, the object. It always has the same name as the class and does not have a return type. To be accessible from another class the constructor needs to be declared in a section marked with the `public` access modifier.

```
class MyRectangle
{
  public:
    int x, y; MyRectangle();
};

MyRectangle::MyRectangle() { x = 10; y = 5; }
```

When a new instance of this class is created the constructor method will be called, which in this case assigns default values to the fields.

```
int main()
{
    MyRectangle s;
}
```

Constructor Overloading

As with any other method the constructor can be overloaded. This will allow an object to be created with different argument lists.

```
class MyRectangle
{
  public:
    int x, y; MyRectangle(); MyRectangle(int, int);
};

MyRectangle::MyRectangle() { x = 10; y = 5; }
MyRectangle::MyRectangle(int a, int b) { x = a; y = b; }
```

For example, with the two constructors defined above the object can be initialized either with no arguments or with two arguments, which will be used to assign the fields.

```
// Calls parameterless constructor
MyRectangle r;

// Calls constructor accepting two integers
MyRectangle t(2,3);
```

C++11 added the ability for constructors to call other constructors. Using this feature the parameterless constructor created earlier is here redefined to call the second constructor.

```
MyRectangle::MyRectangle(): MyRectangle(10, 5);
```

This keyword

Inside the constructor, as well as in other methods belonging to the object – so called *instance methods*– a special keyword called this can be used. This is a pointer to the current instance of the class. It can be useful if, for example, the constructor's parameter names are the same as the field names. The fields can then still be accessed by using the this pointer, even though they are overshadowed by the parameters.

```
MyRectangle::MyRectangle(int x, int y)
{
    this->x = x; this->y = y;
}
```

Field Initialization

As an alternative to assigning fields inside the constructor, they may also be assigned by using the *constructor initialization list*. This list starts with a colon after the constructor parameters, followed by calls to the field's own constructors. This is actually the recommended way of assigning fields through a constructor, because it gives better performance than assigning the fields inside the constructor.

```
MyRectangle::MyRectangle(int a, int b) : x(a), y(b) {}
```

Fields can also be assigned an initial value in their class definition, a convenient feature that was added in C++11. This value is automatically assigned when a new instance is created, before the constructor is run. As such, this assignment can be used to specify a default value for a field that may be overridden in the constructor.

```
class MyRectangle
{
  public:
    // Class member initialization
      int x = 10;
      int y = 5;
};
```

Default Constructor

If no constructors are defined for a class the compiler will automatically create a default parameter less constructor when the program compiles. Because of this, a class can be instantiated even if no constructor has been implemented. The default constructor will only allocate memory for the object. It will not initialize the fields. In contrast to global variables, fields in C++ are not automatically initialized to their default values. The fields will contain whatever garbage is left in their memory locations until they are explicitly assigned values.

Destructor

In addition to constructors, a class can also have an explicitly defined *destructor*. The destructor is used to release any resources allocated by the object. It is called automatically before an object is destroyed, either when the object passes out of scope or when it is explicitly deleted for objects created with the new operator. The name of the destructor is the same as the class name, but preceded by a tilde (~). A class may only have one destructor and it never takes any arguments or returns anything.

```
class Semaphore
{
  public:
    bool *sem;

    Semaphore()  { sem = new bool; }
    ~Semaphore() { delete sem; }
};
```

Special Member Functions

The default constructor and the destructor are both special member functions that the compiler will automatically provide for any class that do not explicitly define them. Two more such methods are the copy constructor and the copy assignment operator (operator =). With the C++11 standard came ways of controlling whether to allow these special member functions or not through the delete and default specifiers. The delete specifier forbids the calling of a function, while the default specifier explicitly states that the compiler-generated default will be used.

```
class A
{
  public:
    // Explicitly include default constructor
  A() = default;
  A(int i);

  // Disable copy constructor
  A(const A&) = delete;

  // Disable copy assignment operator
  A& operator=(const A&) = delete;
};
```

Object Initialization

C++ provides a number of different ways to create objects and initialize their fields. The following class will be used to illustrate these methods.

```
class MyClass
{
public:
int i;
  MyClass() = default;
  MyClass(int x) : i(x) {}
};
```

Direct Initialization

The object creation syntax that has been used so far is called *direct initialization*. This syntax can include a set of parentheses which are used to pass arguments to a constructor in the class. If the parameterless constructor is used, the parentheses are left out.

```
// Direct initialization
MyClass a(5); MyClass b;
```

Value Initialization

An object can also be *value initialized*. The object is then created by using the class name followed by a set of parentheses. The parentheses can supply constructor arguments, or remain empty to construct the object using the parameterless constructor. A value initialization creates only a temporary object, which is destroyed at the end of the statement. To preserve the object it must either be copied to another object or assigned to a reference. Assigning the temporary object to a reference will maintain the object until that reference goes out of scope.

```
// Value initialization
const MyClass& a = MyClass();
MyClass&& b = MyClass();
```

A value initialized object is almost identical to one created by using default initialization. A minor difference is that non-static fields will in some cases be initialized to their default values when using value initialization.

Copy Initialization

If an existing object is assigned to an object of the same type when it is declared, the new object will be *copy initialized*. This means that each member of the existing object will be copied to the new object.

```
// Copy initialization
MyClass a = MyClass();
MyClass b(a);
MyClass c = b;
```

This works because of the implicit *copy constructor* that the compiler provides, which is called for these kinds of assignments. The copy constructor takes a single argument of its own type, and then constructs a copy of the specified object. Note that this behavior is different from many other languages, such as Java and C#. In those languages initializing an object with another object will only copy the object's reference, and not create a new object copy.

New Initialization

An object can be initialized through dynamic memory allocation by using the new keyword. Dynamically allocated memory must be used through a pointer or reference. The new operator returns a pointer, so to assign it to a reference it needs to be dereferenced first. Keep in mind that dynamically allocated memory must be explicitly freed once it is no longer needed.

```
// New initialization
MyClass* a = new MyClass(); MyClass& b = *new MyClass();
// ...
delete a, b;
```

Aggregate Initialization

There is a syntactical shortcut available when initializing an object called *aggregate initialization*. This syntax allows fields to be set by using a brace-enclosed list of initializers, in the same way as can be done with arrays. Aggregate initialization can only be used when the class type does not include any constructors, virtual functions or base classes. The fields must also be public, unless they are declared as static. Each field will be set in the order they appear in the class.

```
// Aggregate initialization
MyClassa = { 2 }; // iis 2
```

Uniform Initialization

The uniform initialization was introduced in C++11 to provide a consistent way to initialize types that works the same for any type. This syntax looks the same as aggregate initialization, without the use of the equal sign.

```
// Uniform initialization
MyClass a { 3 }; // i is 3
```

This initialization syntax works not just for classes but for any type, including primitives, strings, arrays, and standard library containers such as vector.

```
#include <string>
#include <vector>
using namespace std;

int i { 1 };
string s {"Hello"};
int a[] { 1, 2 };
int *p= new int [2] { 1, 2 };
vector<string> box { "one", "two" };
```

Uniform initialization can be used to call a constructor. This is done automatically by passing along the proper arguments for that constructor.

```
// Call parameterless constructor
MyClass b {};
```

```
// Call copy constructor
MyClass c { b };
```

A class can define an initializer-list-constructor. This constructor is called during uniform initialization and takes priority over other forms of construction, provided that the type specified for the initializer_list template matches the type of the brace-enclosed list of arguments. The argument list can be any length but all elements must be of the same type. In the following example the type of the list is int and so the integer list used to construct this object is passed to the constructor. These integers are then displayed using a range-based for loop.

```cpp
#include <iostream>
using namespace std;

class NewClass
{
 public:
  NewClass(initializer_list<int> args)
  {
    for (auto x : args)
      cout << x << " ";
  }
};

int main()
{
  NewClass a { 1, 2, 3 }; // "1 2 3"
}
```

■ ■ ■

CHAPTER 14

Inheritance

Inheritance allows a class to acquire the members of another class. In the example below, Square inherits from Rectangle. This is specified after the class name by using a colon followed by the public keyword, and the name of the class to inherit from. Rectangle then becomes a base class of Square, which in turn becomes a derived class of Rectangle. In addition to its own members, Square gains all accessible members in Rectangle, except for its constructors and destructor.

```cpp
class Rectangle
{
  public:
    int x, y;
    int getArea() { return x * y; }
};

class Square : public Rectangle {};
```

Upcasting

An object can be upcast to its base class, because it contains everything that the base class contains. An upcast is performed by assigning the object to either a reference or a pointer of its base class type. In the example below, a Square object is upcast to Rectangle. When using Rectangle's interface the Square object will be viewed as a Rectangle, so only Rectangle's members can be accessed.

```cpp
Square s;
Rectangle& r = s;  // reference upcast
Rectangle* p = &s; // pointer upcast
```

A derived class can be used anywhere a base class is expected. For example, a Square object can be passed as an argument to a function that expects a Rectangle object. The derived object will then implicitly be upcast to its base type.

```
void setXY(Rectangle& r) { r.x = 2; r.y = 3; }

int main()
{
  Square s;
  setXY(s);
}
```

Downcasting

A Rectangle reference that points to a Square object can be downcast back to a Square object. This downcast has to be made explicit since downcasting an actual Rectangle to a Square is not allowed.

```
Square& a = (Square&) r;   // reference downcast
Square& b = (Square&) *p; // pointer downcast
```

Constructor Inheritance

To make sure the fields in the base class are properly initialized, the parameterless constructor of the base class is automatically called when an object of the derived class is created.

```
class B1
{
 public:
  int x;
  B1() : x(5) {}
};

class D1 : public B1 {};

int main()
{
 // Calls parameterless constructors of D1 and B1
 D1 d;
 cout << d.x; // "5"
}
```

This call to the base constructor can be made explicitly from the derived constructor, by placing it in the constructor's initialization list. This allows arguments to be passed along to the base constructor.

```
class B2
{
 public:
  int x;
  B2(int a) : x(a) {}
};

class D2 : public B2
{
 public:
  D2(int i) : B2(i) {} // call base constructor
};
```

An alternative solution in this case is to inherit the constructor. As of C++11, this can be done through a using statement.

```
class D2 : public B2
{
 public:
  using B2::B2; // inherit all constructors
  int y{0};
};
```

Note that the base class constructor cannot initialize fields defined in the derived class. Therefore, any fields declared in the derived class should initialize themselves. This is done here using the uniform notation.

Multiple Inheritance

C++ allows a derived class to inherit from more than one base class. This is called *multiple inheritance*. The base classes are specified in a comma-separated list.

```
class Person {}
class Employee {}

class Teacher: public Person, public Employee {}
```

Multiple inheritance is not commonly used since most real-world relationships can be better described by single inheritance. It also tends to significantly increase the complexity of the code.

CHAPTER 15

Overriding

A new method in a derived class can redefine a method in a base class in order to give it a new implementation.

Hiding Derived Members

In the example below, Rectangle's getArea method is redeclared in Triangle with the same signature. The signature includes the name, parameter list and return type of the method.

```cpp
class Rectangle
{
 public:
   int x, y;
   int getArea() { return x * y; }
};

class Triangle : public Rectangle
{
 public:
   Triangle(int a, int b) { x = a; y = b; }
   int getArea() { return x * y / 2; }
};
```

If a Triangle object is created and the getArea method is invoked, then Triangle's version of the method will get called.

```cpp
Triangle t = Triangle(2,3);
t.getArea(); // 3 (2*3/2) calls Triangle's version
```

However, if the Triangle is upcast to a Rectangle then Rectangle's version will get called instead.

```cpp
Rectangle& r = t;
r.getArea(); // 6 (2*3) calls Rectangle's version
```

That is because the redefined method has only hidden the inherited method. This means that Triangle's implementation is redefined downwards in the class hierarchy to any child classes of Triangle, but not upwards to the base class.

Overriding Derived Members

In order to redefine a method upwards in the class hierarchy – what is called *overriding* – the method needs to be declared with the virtual modifier in the base class. This modifier allows the method to be overridden in derived classes.

```
class Rectangle
{
 public:
  int x, y;
  virtual int getArea() { return x * y; }
};
```

Calling the getArea method from Rectangle's interface will now invoke Triangle's implementation.

```
Rectangle& r = t;
r.getArea(); // 3 (2*3/2) calls Triangle's version
```

C++11 added the override specifier, which indicates that a method is intended to replace an inherited method. Using this specifier allows the compiler to check that there is a virtual method with that same signature. This prevents the possibility of accidentally creating a new virtual method.

```
virtual float getArea() override {} // error - no base class method to
override
```

Another specifier introduced in C++11 is final. This specifier prevents a virtual method from being overridden in derived classes. It also prevents derived classes from using that same method signature.

```
class Base
{
  virtual void foo() final {}
}

class Derived
{
  void foo() {} // error: Base::foo marked as final
}
```

The final specifier can also be applied to a class to prevent any class from inheriting it.

```
class B final {}
class D : B {} // error: B marked as final
```

Base Class Scoping

It is still possible to access a redefined method from a derived class by typing the class name followed by the scope resolution operator. This is called *base class scoping* and can be used to allow access to redefined methods that are any number of levels deep in the class hierarchy.

```
class Triangle : public Rectangle
{
 public:
  Triangle(int a, int b) { x = a; y = b; }
  int getArea() { return Rectangle::getArea() / 2; }
};
```

CHAPTER 16

■ ■ ■

Access Levels

Every class member has an accessibility level that determines where the member will be visible. There are three of them available in C++: public, protected and private. The default access level for class members is private. To change the access level for a section of code, an access modifier is used followed by a colon. Every field or method that comes after this label will have the specified access level, until another access level is set or the class declaration ends.

```
class MyClass
{
  int myPrivate;

 public:
  int myPublic;
  void publicMethod();
};
```

Private Access

All members regardless of their access level are accessible in the class in which they are declared, the enclosing class. This is the only place where private members can be accessed.

```
class MyClass
{
  // Unrestricted access
  public: int myPublic;

  // Defining or derived class only
  protected: int myProtected;

  // Defining class only
  private: int myPrivate;
```

```
  void test()
  {
    myPublic    = 0; // allowed
    myProtected = 0; // allowed
    myPrivate   = 0; // allowed
  }
};
```

Protected Access

A protected member can also be accessed from inside a derived class, but it cannot be reached from an unrelated class.

```
class MyChild : public MyClass
{
  void test()
  {
    myPublic    = 0; // allowed
    myProtected = 0; // allowed
    myPrivate   = 0; // inaccessible
  }
};
```

Public Access

Public access gives unrestricted access from anywhere in the code.

```
class OtherClass
{
  void test(MyClass& c)
  {
    c.myPublic    = 0; // allowed
    c.myProtected = 0; // inaccessible
    c.myPrivate   = 0; // inaccessible
  }
};
```

Access Level Guideline

As a guideline, when choosing an access level it is generally best to use the most restrictive level possible. This is because the more places a member can be accessed, the more places it can be accessed incorrectly, which makes the code harder to debug. Using restrictive access levels will also make it easier to modify the class without breaking the code for any other programmers using that class.

Friend Classes and Functions

A class can be allowed to access the private and protected members of another class by declaring the class a friend. This is done by using the friend modifier. The friend is allowed to access all members in the class where the friend is defined, but not the other way around.

```
class MyClass
{
  int myPrivate;

  // Give OtherClass access
  friend class OtherClass;
};

class OtherClass
{
  void test(MyClass c) { c.myPrivate = 0; } // allowed
};
```

A global function can also be declared as a friend to a class in order to gain the same level of access.

```
class MyClass
{
  int myPrivate;

  // Give myFriend access
  friend void myFriend(MyClass c);
};

void myFriend(MyClass c) { c.myPrivate = 0; } // allowed
```

Public, Protected and Private Inheritance

When a class is inherited in C++ it is possible to change the access level of the inherited members. Public inheritance allows all members to keep their original access level. Protected inheritance reduces the access of public members to protected. Private inheritance restricts all inherited members to private access.

```
class MyChild : private MyClass
{
  // myPublic is private
  // myProtected is private
  // myPrivate is private
};
```

Private is the default inheritance level, although public inheritance is the one that is nearly always used.

CHAPTER 17

Static

The static keyword is used to create class members that exist in only one copy, which belongs to the class itself. These members are shared among all instances of the class. This is different from instance (non-static) members, which are created as new copies for each new object.

Static Fields

A static field (class field) cannot be initialized inside the class like an instance field. Instead it must be defined outside of the class declaration. This initialization will only take place once, and the static field will then remain initialized throughout the life of the application.

```
class MyCircle
{
 public:
   double r;         // instance field (one per object)
   static double pi; // static field (only one copy)
};

double MyCircle::pi = 3.14;
```

To access a static member from outside the class, the name of the class is used followed by the scope resolution operator and the static member. This means that there is no need to create an instance of a class in order to access its static members.

```
int main()
{
   double p = MyCircle::pi;
}
```

Static Methods

In addition to fields, methods can also be declared as static, in which case they can also be called without having to define an instance of the class. However, because a static method is not part of any instance it cannot use instance members. Methods should therefore only be declared static if they perform a generic function that is independent of any instance variables. Instance methods on the other hand, in contrast to static methods, can use both static and instance members.

```
class MyCircle
{
 public:
  double r;          // instance variable (one per object)
  static double pi; // static variable (only one copy)

  double getArea() { return pi * r * r; }
  static double newArea(double a) { return pi * a * a; }
};

int main()
{
  double a = MyCircle::newArea(1);
}
```

Static Local Variables

Local variables inside a function can be declared as static to make the function remember the variable. A static local variable is only initialized once when execution first reaches the declaration, and that declaration is then ignored every subsequent time the execution passes through.

```
int myFunc()
{
  static int count = 0; // holds # of calls to function
  count++;
}
```

Static Global Variables

One last place where the static keyword can be applied is to global variables. This will limit the accessibility of the variable to only the current source file, and can therefore be used to help avoid naming conflicts.

```
// Only visible within this source file
static int myGlobal;
```

CHAPTER 18

Enum

Enum is a user-defined type consisting of a fixed list of named constants. In the example below, the enumeration type is called Color and contains three constants: Red, Green and Blue.

```
enum Color { Red, Green, Blue };
```

The Color type can be used to create variables that may hold one of these constant values.

```
int main()
{
    Color c = Red;
}
```

Enum constants may be prefixed with the enum name for added clarity. However, these constants are always unscoped, and so care must be taken to avoid naming conflicts.

```
Color c = Color::Red;
```

Enum Example

The switch statement provides a good example of when enumerations can be useful. Compared to using ordinary constants, the enumeration has the advantage that it allows the programmer to clearly specify what values a variable should contain.

```
switch(c)
{
    case Red:   break;
    case Green: break;
    case Blue:  break;
}
```

Enum Constant Values

Usually there is no need to know the underlying values that the constants represent, but in some cases it can be useful. By default, the first constant in the enum list has the value zero and each successive constant is one value higher.

```
enum Color
{
    Red    // 0
    Green // 1
    Blue  // 2
};
```

These default values can be overridden by assigning values to the constants. The values can be computed and do not have to be unique.

```
enum Color
{
    Red   = 5,         // 5
    Green = Red,       // 5
    Blue  = Green + 2 // 7
};
```

Enum Conversions

The compiler can implicitly convert an enumeration constant to an integer. However, converting an integer back into an enum variable requires an explicit cast, since this conversion makes it possible to assign a value that is not included in the enum's list of constants.

```
int i = Red;
Color c = (Color)i;
```

Enum Scope

An enum does not have to be declared globally. It can also be placed within a class as a class member, or locally within a function.

```
class MyClass
{
    enum Color { Red, Green, Blue };
};

void myFunction()
{
    enum Color { Red, Green, Blue };
}
```

Strongly Typed Enums

The enum class was introduced in C++11 to provide a safer alternative to the regular enum. These new enums are defined in the same way as regular enums, with the addition of the class keyword.

```
enum class Speed
{
    Fast,
    Normal,
    Slow
};
```

With the new enum the specified constants belong within the scope of the enum class name, as opposed to the outer scope as for regular enums. To access an enum class constant, it must therefore be qualified with the enum name.

```
Speed s = Speed::Fast;
```

The underlying integral type of the regular enum is not defined by the standard and may vary between implementations. In contrast, a class enum always uses the int type by default. This type can be overridden to another integer type, as seen below.

```
enum class MyEnum : unsigned short {};
```

One last important advantage of enum classes is their type safety. Unlike regular enums, enum classes are strongly typed and will therefore not convert implicitly to integer types.

```
if (s == Speed::Fast) {} // ok
if (s == 0) {}            // error
```

CHAPTER 19

Struct and Union

Struct

A struct in C++ is equivalent to a class, except that members of a struct default to public access, instead of private access as in classes. By convention, structs are used instead of classes to represent simple data structures that mainly contain public fields.

```
struct Point
{
    int x, y; // public
};

class Point
{
    int x, y; // private
};
```

Declarator List

To declare objects of a struct the normal declaration syntax can be used.

```
Point p, q; // object declarations
```

Another alternative syntax often used with structs is to declare the objects when the struct is defined by placing the object names before the final semicolon. This position is known as the *declarator list* and can contain a comma-separated sequence of declarators.

```
struct Point
{
    int x, y;
} r, s; // object declarations
```

Aggregate initialization is also commonly used with structs, since this syntactical shortcut only works for simple aggregate types with public fields. For compilers supporting C++11, the uniform initialization syntax is preferred, as it removes the distinction between initialization of aggregate and non-aggregate types.

```
int main()
{
  // Aggregate initialization
  Point p = { 2, 3 };

  // Uniform initialization
  Point q { 2, 3 };
}
```

Union

Although similar to struct, the union type is different in that all fields share the same memory position. Therefore, the size of a union is the size of the largest field it contains. For example, in the case below this is the integer field which is 4 bytes large.

```
union Mix
{
    char c;  // 1 byte
    short s; // 2 bytes
    int i;   // 4 bytes
} m;
```

This means that the union type can only be used to store one value at a time, because changing one field will overwrite the value of the others.

```
int main()
{
    m.c = 0xFF; // set first 8 bits
    m.s = 0;    // reset first 16 bits
}
```

The benefit of a union, in addition to efficient memory usage, is that it provides multiple ways of viewing the same memory location. For example, the union below has three data members that allow access to the same group of 4 bytes in multiple ways.

```
union Mix
{
    char c[4];                    // 4 bytes
    struct { short hi, lo; } s;   // 4 bytes
    int i;                        // 4 bytes
} m;
```

The integer field will access all 4 bytes at once. With the struct 2 bytes can be viewed at a time, and by using the char array each byte can be referenced individually.

```
int main()
{
m.i=0xFF00F00F; // 11111111 00000000 11110000 00001111
m.s.lo;         // 11111111 00000000
m.s.hi;         //                   11110000 00001111
m.c[3];         // 11111111
m.c[2];         //          00000000
m.c[1];         //                   11110000
m.c[0];         //                            00001111}
```

Anonymous Union

A union type can be declared without a name. This is called an *anonymous union* and defines an unnamed object whose members can be accessed directly from the scope where it is declared. An anonymous union cannot contain methods or non-public members.

```
int main()
{
    union { short s; }; // defines an unnamed union object s = 15;
}
```

An anonymous union that is declared globally must be made static.

```
static union {};
```

CHAPTER 20

■ ■ ■

Operator Overloading

Operator overloading allows operators to be redefined and used where one or both of the operands are of a user-defined class. When done correctly, this can simplify the code and make user-defined types as easy to use as the primitive types.

Operator Overloading Example

In the example below there is a class called MyNum with an integer field and a constructor for setting that field. The class also has an addition method that adds two MyNum objects together and returns the result as a new object.

```
class MyNum
{
 public:
   int val;
   MyNum(int i) : val(i) {}

   MyNum add(MyNum &a)
   { return MyNum( val + a.val ); }
}
```

Two MyNum instances can be added together using this method.

```
MyNum a = MyNum(10), b = MyNum(5);
MyNum c = a.add(b);
```

Binary Operator Overloading

What operator overloading does is simplify this syntax and thereby provide a more intuitive interface for the class. To convert the add method to an overload for the addition sign, replace the name of the method with the operator keyword followed by the operator that is to be overloaded. The whitespace between the keyword and the operator can optionally be left out.

```
MyNum operator + (MyNum &a)
{ return MyNum( val + a.val ); }
```

Since the class now overloads the addition sign, this operator can be used to perform the calculation needed.

```
MyNum c = a + b;
```

Keep in mind that the operator is only an alternative syntax for calling the actual method.

```
MyNum d = a.operator + (b);
```

Unary Operator Overloading

Addition is a binary operator, because it takes two operands. The first operand is the object from which the method is called, and the second operand is that which is passed to the method. When overloading a unary operator, such as prefix increment (++), there is no need for a method parameter since these operators only affect the object from which they are called.

With unary operators, a reference of the same type as the object should always be returned. This is because when using a unary operator on an object, programmers expect the result to return the same object and not just a copy. On the other hand, when using a binary operator, programmers expect a copy of the result to be returned and therefore return by value should be used.

```
MyNum& operator++() // ++ prefix
{ ++val; return *this; }
```

Not all unary operators should return by reference. The two postfix operators – post-increment and post-decrement – should instead return by value, because the postfix operations are expected to return the state of the object before the increment or decrement occurs. Note that the postfix operators have an unused int parameter specified. This parameter is used to distinguish them from the prefix operators.

```
MyNum operator++(int) // postfix ++
{
  MyNum t = MyNum(val);
  ++val;
  return t;
}
```

Overloadable Operators

C++ allows overloading of almost all operators in the language. As can be seen in the table below, most operators are of the binary type. Only a few of them are unary, and some special operators cannot be categorized as either. There are also some operators that cannot be overloaded at all.

Binary operators	Unary operators
+ - * / %	+ - ! ~ & * ++ --
= + = - = * = / = % =	**Special operators**
& = ^ = | = << = >> =	( ) [ ] delete new
== != > < > = < =	**Not overloadable**
& | ^ << >> && ||	. .* :: ?: # ## sizeof
-> ->* ,	

CHAPTER 21

■ ■ ■

Custom Conversions

Custom type conversions can be defined to allow an object to be constructed from or converted to another type. In the following example, there is a class called MyNum with a single integer field. With conversion constructors it is possible to allow integer types to be implicitly converted to this object's type.

```
class MyNum
{
  public:
    int value;
};
```

Implicit Conversion Constructor

For this type conversion to work, a constructor needs to be added that takes a single parameter of the desired type, in this case an int.

```
class MyNum
{
  public:
    int value;
    MyNum(int i) { value = i; }
};
```

When an integer is assigned to an object of MyNum this constructor will implicitly be called to perform the type conversion.

```
MyNum A = 5; // implicit conversion
```

This means that any constructor that takes exactly one argument can be used both for constructing objects and for performing implicit type conversions to that object type.

```
MyNum B = MyNum(5); // object construction
MyNum C(5);         // object construction
```

These conversions will work not only for the specific parameter type, but also for any type that can be implicitly converted to it. For example, a char can be implicitly converted to an int and can therefore be implicitly changed into a MyNum object as well.

```
MyNum D = 'H'; // implicit conversion (char->int->MyNum)
```

Explicit Conversion Constructor

To help prevent potentially unintended object type conversions it is possible to disable the second use of the single parameter constructor. The explicit constructor modifier is then applied, which specifies that the constructor may only be used for object construction, and not for type conversion.

```
class MyNum
{
  public:
    int value;
    explicit MyNum(int i) { value = i; }
};
```

The explicit constructor syntax must therefore be used to create a new object.

```
MyNum A = 5;        // error
MyNum B(5);         // allowed
MyNum C = MyNum(5); // allowed
```

Conversion Operators

Custom conversion operators allow conversions to be specified in the other direction: from the object's type to another type. The operator keyword is then used, followed by the target type, a set of parentheses, and a method body. The body returns a value of the target type, in this case int.

```
class MyNum
{
  public:
    int value;
    operator int() { return value; }
};
```

When objects of this class are evaluated in an int context, this conversion operator will be called to perform the type conversion.

```
MyNum A { 5 };
int i = A; // 5
```

Explicit Conversion Operators

The C++11 standard added explicit conversion operators to the language. Similar to explicit constructors, the inclusion of the explicit keyword prevents the conversion operator from being implicitly called.

```
class True
{
  explicit operator bool() const {
    return true;
  }
};
```

The class above provides a safe bool that prevents its objects from mistakenly being used in a mathematical context through the bool conversion operator. In the example below, the first comparison results in a compile error since the bool conversion operator cannot be implicitly called. The second comparison is allowed because the conversion operator is explicitly called through the type cast.

```
True a, b;
if (a == b) {}          // error
if ((bool)a == (bool)b) {} // allowed
```

Bear in mind that contexts requiring a bool value, such as the condition for an if statement, counts as explicit conversions.

```
if (a) {} // allowed
```

CHAPTER 22

■ ■ ■

Namespaces

Namespaces are used to avoid naming conflicts by allowing entities, such as classes and functions, to be grouped under a separate scope. In the example below there are two classes that belong to the global scope. Since both classes share the same name and scope the code will not compile.

```
class Table {};
class Table {}; // error: class type redefinition
```

One way to solve this problem would be to rename one of the conflicting classes. Another solution is to group one or both of them under a different namespace by enclosing each in a namespace block. The classes then belong to different scopes and so will no longer cause a naming conflict.

```
namespace furniture
{
    class Table {};
}

namespace html
{
    class Table {};
}
```

Accessing Namespace Members

To access a member of a namespace from outside that namespace the member's fully qualified name needs to be specified. This means that the member name has to be prefixed with the namespace it belongs to, followed by the scope resolution operator.

```
int main()
{
    furniture::Table fTable;
    html::Table hTable;
}
```

Nesting Namespaces

It is possible to nest namespaces any number of levels deep to further structure the program entities.

```
namespace furniture
{
    namespace wood { class Table {}; }
}
```

Ensure that the nested namespace members are qualified with the full namespace hierarchy when using them from another namespace.

```
furniture::wood::Table fTable;
```

Importing Namespaces

To avoid having to specify the namespace every time one of its members is used, the namespace can be imported into the global or local scope with the help of a using declaration. This declaration includes the using namespace keywords followed by the namespace to be imported. It can be placed either locally or globally. Locally, the declaration will only be in scope until the end of the code block, while at the global scope it will apply to the whole source file following its declaration.

```
using namespace html;    // global namespace import
int main()
{
    using namespace html; // local namespace import
}
```

Keep in mind that importing a namespace into the global scope defeats the main purpose of using namespaces, which is to avoid naming conflicts. Such conflicts however are mainly an issue in projects that use several independently developed code libraries.

Namespace Member Import

If you want to avoid both typing the fully qualified name and importing the whole namespace there is a third alternative available. That is to only import the specific members that are needed from the namespace. This is done by declaring one member at a time with the using keyword followed by the fully qualified namespace member to be imported.

```
using html::Table; // import a single namespace member
```

Namespace Alias

Another way to shorten the fully qualified name is to create a namespace alias. The namespace keyword is then used followed by an alias name, to which the fully qualified namespace is assigned.

```
namespace myAlias = furniture::wood; // namespace alias
```

This alias can then be used instead of the namespace qualifier that it represents.

```
myAlias::Table fTable;
```

Note that both the namespace member imports and the namespace aliases may be declared both globally and locally.

Type Alias

Aliases can also be created for types. A type alias is defined using the typedef keyword followed by the type and the alias.

```
typedef my::name::MyClass MyType;
```

The alias can then be used as a synonym for the specified type.

```
MyType t;
```

Typedef does not only work for existing types, but can also include a definition of a user-defined type – such as a class, struct, union or enum.

```
typedef struct { int len; } Length;
Length a, b, c;
```

C++11 added a using statement that provides a more intuitive syntax for aliasing types. With this syntax the keyword using is followed by the alias name and then assigned the type. Unlike typedef the using statement also allows templates to be aliased.

```
using MyType = my::name::MyClass;
```

Aliases are not commonly used since they tend to obfuscate the code. However, if used properly a type alias can simplify a long or confusing type name. Another function they provide is the ability to change the definition of a type from a single location.

Including Namespace Members

Keep in mind that in C++ merely importing a namespace does not provide access to the members included in that namespace. In order to access the namespace members the prototypes also have to be made available, for example by using the appropriate #include directives.

```
// Include input/output prototypes
#include <iostream>

// Import standard library namespace to global scope using namespace std;
```

CHAPTER 23

Constants

A constant is a variable that has a value which cannot be changed once the constant has been assigned. This allows the compiler to enforce that the variable's value is not changed anywhere in the code by mistake.

Constant Variables

A variable can be made into a constant by adding the const keyword either before or after the data type. This modifier means that the variable becomes read-only, and it must therefore be assigned a value at the same time as it is declared. Attempting to change the value anywhere else results in a compile-time error.

```
const int var = 5;
int const var2 = 10; // alternative order
```

Constant Pointers

When it comes to pointers, const can be used in two ways. First, the pointer can be made constant, which means that it cannot be changed to point to another location.

```
int myPointee;
int* const p = &myPointee; // pointer constant
```

Second, the pointee can be declared constant. This means that the variable pointed to cannot be modified through this pointer.

```
const int* q = &var; // pointee constant
```

It is possible to declare both the pointer and the pointee as constant to make them both read-only.

```
const int* const r = &var; // pointer & pointee constant
```

Note that constant variables may not be pointed to by a non-constant pointer. This prevents programmers from accidentally rewriting a constant variable using a pointer.

```
int* s = &var; // error: const to non-const assignment
```

Constant References

References can be declared constant in the same way as pointers. However, since reseating a reference is never allowed, declaring the reference as const would be redundant. It only makes sense to protect the referee from change.

```
const int& y = var; // referee constant
```

Constant Objects

Just as with variables, pointers and references, objects can also be declared constant. Take the following class as an example.

```
class MyClass
{
  public: int x;
  void setX(int a) { x = a; }
};
```

A constant object of this class cannot be reassigned to another instance.

The constness of an object also affects its fields and prevent them from being changed.

```
const MyClass a, b;
a = b;    // error: object is const
a.x = 10; // error: object field is const
```

Constant Methods

Because of this last restriction, a constant object may not call a non-constant method since such methods are allowed to change the object's fields.

```
a.setX(2); // error: cannot call non-const method
```

They may only call constant methods, which are methods that are marked with the const modifier before the method body.

```
int getX() const { return x; } // constant method
```

This const modifier means that the method is not allowed to modify the state of the object and can therefore safely be called by a constant object of the class. More specifically, the const modifier applies to the this pointer that is implicitly passed to the method. This effectively restricts the method from modifying the object's fields or calling any non-constant methods in the class.

Constant Return Type and Parameters

In addition to making a method constant, the return type and method parameters may also be made read-only. For example, if a field is returned by reference instead of by value from a constant method it is important that it is returned as a constant in order to maintain the constness of the object. Not all C++ compilers will be able to catch this subtle mistake.

```
const int& getX() const { return x; }
```

Constant Fields

Both static and instance fields in a class can be declared constant. A constant instance field must be assigned its value using the constructor initialization list. This is the same as the preferred way of initializing regular (non-constant, non-static) fields.

```
class MyClass
{
 public:
   int i;
   const int c;
   MyClass() : c(5), i(5) {}
}
```

A constant static field has to be defined outside of the class declaration, in the same way as non-constant static fields. The exception to this is when the constant static field is of an integer data type. Such a field may also be initialized within the class at the same time as the field is declared.

```
class MyClass
{
 public:
   static int si;
   const static double csd;
   const static int csi = 5;
};
int MyClass::si = 1.23;
const double MyClass::csd = 1.23;
```

Constant Expressions

The keyword constexpr was introduced in C++11 to indicate a constant expression. Like const it can be applied to variables to make them constant, causing a compilation error if any code attempts to modify the value.

```
constexpr int myConst = 5;
myConst = 3; // error: variable is const
```

Unlike const variables, which may be assigned at runtime, a constant expression variable will be computed at compile time. Such a variable can therefore always be used where a compile-time constant is needed, such as in an array and enum declarations. Prior to C++11, this was only allowed for constant integer and enumeration types.

```
int myArray[myConst + 1];
```

Functions and class constructors may also be defined as constant expressions, which is not allowed with const. Using constexpr on a function limits what the function is allowed to do. In short, the function must consist of a single return statement, and it can only reference other constexpr functions and global constexpr variables. C++14 relaxes these constraints, allowing constexpr functions to contain other executable statements.

```
constexpr int getDefaultSize(int multiplier)
{
  return 3 * multiplier;
}
```

The return value for a constexpr function is guaranteed to be evaluated at compile time only when its arguments are constant expressions and the return value is used where a compile-time constant is necessary.

```
// Compile-time evaluation
int myArray[getDefaultSize(10)];
```

If the function is called without constant arguments, it returns a value at runtime just like a regular function.

```
// Run-time call
int mul = 10;
int size = getDefaultSize(mul);
```

Constructors can be declared with constexpr, to construct a constant expression object. Such a constructor must be trivial.

```
class Circle
{
public:
    int r;
    constexpr Circle(int x) : r(x) {}
};
```

When called with a constant expression argument, the result will be a compile-time generated object with read-only fields. With other arguments it will behave as an ordinary constructor.

```
// Compile-time object
constexpr Circle c1(5);

// Run-time object
int x = 5;
Circle c2(x);
```

Constant Guideline

In general, it is a good idea to always declare variables as constants if they do not need to be modified. This ensures that the variables are not changed anywhere in the program by mistake, which in turn will help to prevent bugs. There is also a performance gain by allowing the compiler the opportunity to hard-code constant expressions into the compiled program. This allows the expression to be evaluated only once – during compilation – rather than every time the program runs.

CHAPTER 24

▮ ▮ ▮

Preprocessor

The preprocessor is a text substitution tool that modifies the source code before the compilation takes place. This modification is done according to the preprocessor directives that are included in the source files. The directives are easily distinguished from normal programming code in that they all start with a hash sign (#). They must always appear as the first non-whitespace character on a line, and they do not end with a semicolon. The following table shows the preprocessor directives available in C++ along with their functions.

Directive	Description
#include	File include
#define	Macro definition
#undef	Macro undefine
#ifdef	If macro defined
#ifndef	If macro not defined
#if	If
#elif	Else if
#else	Else
#endif	End if
#line	Set line number
#error	Abort compilation
#pragma	Set compiler option

Including Source Files

The #include directive inserts the contents of a file into the current source file. Its most common use is to include header files, both user-defined and library ones. Library header files are enclosed between angle brackets (<>). This tells the preprocessor to search for the header in the default directory where it is configured to look for standard header files.

```
#include <iostream> // search library directory
```

Header files that you create for your own program are enclosed within double quotes (""). The preprocessor will then search for the file in the same directory as the current file. In case the header is not found there, the preprocessor will then search among the standard header files.

```
#include "MyFile.h" // search current, then default
```

The double quoted form can also be used to specify an absolute or relative path to the file.

```
#include "C:\MyFile.h" // absolute path
#include "..\MyFile.h" // relative path
```

Define

Another important directive is #define, which is used to create compile-time constants, also called macros. After this directive, the name of the constant is specified followed by what it will be replaced by.

```
#define PI 3.14 // macro definition
```

The preprocessor will go through and change any occurrences of this constant with whatever comes after it in its definition until the end of the line.

```
float f = PI; // f = 3.14
```

By convention, constants should be named in uppercase letters with each word separated by an underscore. That way they are easy to spot when reading the source code.

Undefine

A #define directive should not be used to directly override a previously defined macro. Doing so will give a compiler warning. In order to change a macro, it first needs to be undefined using the #undef directive. Attempting to undefine a macro that is not currently defined will not generate a warning.

```
#undef PI // undefine
#undef PI // allowed
```

Predefined Macros

There are a number of macros that are predefined by the compiler. To distinguish them from other macros, their names begin and end with two underscores. These standard macros are listed in the following table.

Directive	Description
__FILE__	Name and path for the current file.
__LINE__	Current line number.
__DATE__	Compilation date in MM DD YYYY format.
__TIME__	Compilation time in HH:MM:SS format.
__func__	Name of the current function. Added in C++11.

A common use for predefined macros is to provide debugging information. To give an example, the following error message includes the file name and line number where the message occurs.

```
cout << "Error in " << __FILE__ << " at line " << __LINE__;
```

Macro Functions

Macros can be made to take arguments. This allows them to define compile-time functions. For example, the following macro function gives the square of its argument.

```
#define SQUARE(x) ((x)*(x))
```

The macro function is called just as if it was a regular C++ function. Keep in mind that for this kind of function to work, the arguments must be known at compile time.

```
int x = SQUARE(2); // 4
```

Note the extra parentheses in the macro definition that are used to avoid problems with operator precedence. Without the parentheses the following example would give an incorrect result, as the multiplication would then be carried out before the addition.

```
#define SQUARE(x) x*x

int main(void) {
  int x = SQUARE(1+1); // 1+1*1+1 = 3
}
```

To break a macro function across several lines the backslash character can be used. This will escape the newline character that marks the end of a preprocessor directive. For this to work there must not be any whitespace after the backslash.

```
#define MAX(a,b)  \
a>b ? \
a:b
```

Although macros can be powerful, they tend to make the code more difficult to read and debug. Macros should therefore only be used when they are absolutely necessary and should always be kept short. C++ code such as constant variables, enum classes, and constexpr functions can often accomplish the same goal more efficiently and safely than #define directives can.

```
#define DEBUG 0
const bool DEBUG = 0;

#define FORWARD 1
#define STOP 0
#define BACKWARD -1
enum class DIR { FORWARD = 1, STOP = 0, BACKWARD = -1 };

#define MAX(a,b) a>b ? a:b
constexpr int MAX(int a, int b) { return a>b ? a:b; }
```

Conditional Compilation

The directives used for conditional compilation can include or exclude part of the source code if a certain condition is met. First, there is the #if and #endif directives, which specifies a section of code that will only be included if the condition after the #if directive is true. Note that this condition must evaluate to a constant expression.

```
#define DEBUG_LEVEL 3

#if DEBUG_LEVEL > 2
 // ...
#endif
```

Just as with the C++ if statement, any number of #elif (else if) directives and one final #else directive can be included.

```
#if DEBUG_LEVEL > 2
 // ...
#elif DEBUG_LEVEL == 2
 // ...
#else
 // ...
#endif
```

Conditional compilation also provides a useful means of temporarily commenting out large blocks of code for testing purposes. This often cannot be done with the regular multiline comment since they cannot be nested.

```
#if 0
 /* Removed from compilation */
#endif
```

Compile if Defined

Sometimes, a section of code should only be compiled if a certain macro has been defined, irrespective of its value. For this purpose two special operators can be used: defined and !defined (not defined).

```
#define DEBUG

#if defined DEBUG
 // ...
#elif !defined DEBUG
 // ...
#endif
```

The same effect can also be achieved using the directives #ifdef and #ifndef respectively. For instance, the #ifdef section is only compiled if the specified macro has been previously defined. Note that a macro is considered defined even if it has not been given a value.

```
#ifdef DEBUG
 // ...
#endif

#ifndef DEBUG
 // ...
#endif
```

Error

When the #error directive is encountered the compilation is aborted. This directive can be useful to determine whether or not a certain line of code is being compiled. It can optionally take a parameter that specifies the description of the generated compilation error.

```
#error Compilation aborted
```

Line

A less commonly used directive is #line, which can change the line number that is displayed when an error occurs during compilation. Following this directive the line number will as usual be increased by one for each successive line. The directive can take an optional string parameter that sets the filename that will be shown when an error occurs.

```
#line 5 "myapp.cpp"
```

Pragma

The last standard directive is #pragma, or pragmatic information. This directive is used to specify options to the compiler; and as such, they are vendor specific. To give an example, #pragma message can be used with many compilers to output a string to the build window. Another common argument for this directive is warning, which changes how the compiler handles warnings.

```
// Show compiler message
#pragma message( "Hello Compiler" )

// Disable warning 4507
#pragma warning(disable : 4507)
```

Attributes

A new standardized syntax was introduced in C++11 for providing compiler specific information in the source code, so-called attributes. Attributes are placed within double square brackets and may, depending on the attribute, be applied to any code entities. To give an example, a standard attribute added in C++14 is [[deprecated]], which indicates that use of a code entity has become discouraged.

```
// Mark as deprecated
[[deprecated]] void foo() {}
```

This attribute allows the compiler to emit a warning whenever such an entity is used. A message can be included in this warning, to describe why the entity has been deprecated.

```
[[deprecated("foo() is unsafe, use bar() instead")]]
void foo() {}
```

CHAPTER 25

■ ■ ■

Exception Handling

Exception handling allows programmers to deal with unexpected situations that may occur in a program.

Throwing Exceptions

When a function encounters a situation that it cannot recover from it can generate an exception to signal the caller that the function has failed. This is done using the throw keyword followed by whatever it is the function wants to signal. When this statement is reached, the function will stop executing and the exception will propagate up to the caller where it can be caught, using a try-catch statement.

```
nt divide(int x, int y)
{
  if (y == 0) throw 0;
  return x / y;
}
```

Try-catch statement

The try-catch statement consists of a try block containing code that may cause exceptions and one or more catch clauses to handle them. In the above case an integer is thrown and so a catch block needs to be included that handles this type of exception. The thrown expression will get passed as an argument to this exception handler, where it can be used to determine what has gone wrong with the function. Note that when the exception has been handled, the execution will then continue running after the try-catch blocks and not after the throw statement.

```
try {
  divide(10,0);
}
catch(int& e) {
  std::cout << "Error code: " << e;
}
```

An exception handler can catch a thrown expression by either value, reference or pointer. However, catching by value should be avoided since this causes an extra copy to be made. Catching by reference is generally preferable. If the code in the try block can throw more types of exceptions then more catch clauses need to be added to handle them as well. Keep in mind that only the handler that matches the thrown expression will be executed.

```
catch(char& e) {
  std::cout << "Error char: " << e;
}
```

To catch all types of exceptions an ellipsis (. . .) can be used as the parameter of catch. This default handler must be placed as the last catch statement since no handler placed after it will ever be executed.

```
catch(...) { std::cout << "Error"; }
```

Re-throwing Exceptions

If an exception handler is not able to recover from an exception it can be re-thrown by using the throw keyword with no argument specified. This will pass the exception up the caller stack until another try-catch block is encountered. Be careful however, because if an exception is never caught the program will terminate with a run-time error.

```
int main()
{
  try {
    try { throw 0; }
    catch(...) { throw; } // re-throw exception
  }
  catch(...) { throw; }   // run-time error
}
```

Exception Specification

Functions are by default allowed to throw exceptions of any type. To specify the exception types that a function may throw the throw keyword can be appended to the function declaration. The throw keyword is followed by a comma separated list of the allowed types, if any, enclosed in parentheses.

```
void error1() {}            // may throw any exceptions
void error2() throw(...) {} // may throw any exceptions
void error3() throw(int) {} // may only throw int
void error4() throw() {}     // may not throw exceptions
```

This kind of exception specification is very different from the one used in for example Java, and overall there is very little reason to specify exceptions in C++. The compiler will not enforce the specified exceptions in any way and it will not be able to make any optimizations because of them.

Use of throw for exception specification was deprecated in C++11 and replaced by a noexcept specifier. Similar to throw(), this specifier indicates that a function is intended not to throw any exceptions. The main difference is that noexcept enables certain compiler optimizations, because the specifier allows the program to terminate without unwinding the call stack if for any reason an exception still occurs.

```
void foo() noexcept {} // may not throw exceptions
```

Exception Class

As previously mentioned, any data type can be thrown in C++. However, the standard library does provide a base class called exception which is specifically designed to declare objects to be thrown. It is defined in the exception header file and is located under the std namespace. As seen below, the class can be constructed with a string that becomes the exception's description.

```
#include <exception>
void make_error()
{
  throw std::exception("My Error Description");
}
```

When catching this exception the object's function what can be used to retrieve the description.

```
try { make_error(); }
catch (std::exception e) {
  std::cout << e.what();
}
```

CHAPTER 26

Type Conversions

Converting an expression from one type to another is known as type-conversion. This can be done either implicitly or explicitly.

Implicit Conversions

An implicit conversion is performed automatically by the compiler when an expression needs to be converted into one of its compatible types. For example, any conversions between the primitive data types can be done implicitly.

```
long a = 5;   // int implicitly converted to long
double b = a; // long implicitly converted to double
```

These implicit primitive conversions can be further grouped into two kinds: *promotion* and *demotion*. Promotion occurs when an expression gets implicitly converted into a larger type and demotion occurs when converting an expression to a smaller type. Because a demotion can result in the loss of information, these conversions will generate a warning on most compilers. If the potential information loss is intentional, the warning can be suppressed by using an explicit cast.

```
// Promotion
long   a = 5;  // int promoted to long
double b = a;  // long promoted to double

// Demotion
int  c = 10.5; // warning: possible loss of data
bool d = c;    // warning: possible loss of data
```

Explicit Conversions

The first explicit cast is the one inherited from C, commonly called the *C-style cast*. The desired data type is simply placed in parentheses to the left of the expression that needs to be converted.

```
int  c = (int)10.5; // double demoted to int
char d = (char)c;   // int demoted to char
```

C++ casts

The C-style cast is suitable for most conversions between the primitive data types. However, when it comes to conversions between classes and pointers it can be too powerful. In order to get greater control over the different types of conversions possible C++ introduced four new casts, called *named casts* or *new-style casts*. These casts are: static, reinterpret, const and dynamic cast.

```
static_cast<new_type> (expression)
reinterpret_cast<new_type> (expression)
const_cast<new_type> (expression)
dynamic_cast<new_type> (expression)
```

As seen above, their format is to follow the cast's name with the new type enclosed in angle brackets and thereafter the expression to be converted in parentheses. These casts allow more precise control over how a conversion should be performed, which in turn makes it easier for the compiler to catch conversion errors. In contrast, the C-style cast includes the static, reinterpret and const cast in one operation. That cast is therefore more likely to execute subtle conversion errors if used incorrectly.

Static Cast

The static cast performs conversions between compatible types. It is similar to the C-style cast, but is more restrictive. For example, the C-style cast would allow an integer pointer to point to a char.

```
char c = 10;       // 1 byte
int *p = (int*)&c; // 4 bytes
```

Since this results in a 4-byte pointer pointing to 1 byte of allocated memory, writing to this pointer will either cause a run-time error or will overwrite some adjacent memory.

```
*p = 5; // run-time error: stack corruption
```

In contrast to the C-style cast, the static cast will allow the compiler to check that the pointer and pointee data types are compatible, which allows the programmer to catch this incorrect pointer assignment during compilation.

```
int *q = static_cast<int*>(&c); // compile-time error
```

Reinterpret Cast

To force the pointer conversion, in the same way as the C-style cast does in the background, the reinterpret cast would be used instead.

```
int *r = reinterpret_cast<int*>(&c); // forced conversion
```

This cast handles conversions between certain unrelated types, such as from one pointer type to another incompatible pointer type. It will simply perform a binary copy of the data without altering the underlying bit pattern. Note that the result of such a low-level operation is system-specific and therefore not portable. It should be used with caution if it cannot be avoided altogether.

Const Cast

The third C++ cast is the const cast. This one is primarily used to add or remove the const modifier of a variable.

```
const int myConst = 5;
int *nonConst = const_cast<int*>(&a); // removes const
```

Although const cast allows the value of a constant to be changed, doing so is still invalid code that may cause a run-time error. This could occur for example if the constant was located in a section of read-only memory.

```
*nonConst = 10; // potential run-time error
```

Const cast is instead used mainly when there is a function that takes a non-constant pointer argument, even though it does not modify the pointee.

```
void print(int *p) { std::cout << *p; }
```

The function can then be passed a constant variable by using a const cast.

```
print(&myConst); // error: cannot convert
                 // const int* to int*

print(nonConst); // allowed
```

C-style and New-Style Casts

Keep in mind that the C-style cast can also remove the const modifier, but again since it does this conversion behind the scenes the C++ casts are preferable. Another reason to use the C++ casts is that they are easier to find in the source code then the C-style cast. This is important because casting errors can be difficult to discover. A third reason for using the C++ casts is that they are unpleasant to write. Since explicit conversion in many cases can be avoided, this was done intentionally so that programmers would look for a different solution.

Dynamic Cast

The fourth and final C++ cast is the dynamic cast. This one is only used to convert object pointers and object references into other pointer or reference types in the inheritance hierarchy. It is the only cast that makes sure that the object pointed to can be converted, by performing a run-time check that the pointer refers to a complete object of the destination type. For this run-time check to be possible the object must be *polymorphic*. That is, the class must define or inherit at least one virtual function. This is because the compiler will only generate the needed run-time type information for such objects.

Dynamic Cast Examples

In the example below, a MyChild pointer is converted into a MyBase pointer using a dynamic cast. This derived-to-base conversion succeeds, because the Child object includes a complete Base object.

```
class MyBase { public: virtual void test() {} };
class MyChild : public MyBase {};

int main()
{
  MyChild *child = new MyChild();
  MyBase  *base = dynamic_cast<MyBase*>(child); // ok
}
```

The next example attempts to convert a MyBase pointer to a MyChild pointer. Since the Base object does not contain a complete Child object this pointer conversion will fail. To indicate this, the dynamic cast returns a null pointer. This gives a convenient way to check whether or not a conversion has succeeded during run-time.

```
MyBase  *base = new MyBase();
MyChild *child = dynamic_cast<MyChild*>(base);

if (child == 0) std::cout << "Null pointer returned";
```

If a reference is converted instead of a pointer, the dynamic cast will then fail by throwing a bad_cast exception. This needs to be handled using a try-catch statement.

```
#include <exception>
// ...
try { MyChild &child = dynamic_cast<MyChild&>(*base); }
catch(std::bad_cast &e)
{
  std::cout << e.what(); // bad dynamic_cast
}
```

Dynamic or Static Cast

The advantage of using a dynamic cast is that it allows the programmer to check whether or not a conversion has succeeded during run-time. The disadvantage is that there is a performance overhead associated with doing this check. For this reason using a static cast would have been preferable in the first example, because a derived-to-base conversion will never fail.

```
MyBase *base = static_cast<MyBase*>(child); // ok
```

However, in the second example the conversion may either succeed or fail. It will fail if the MyBase object contains a MyBase instance and it will succeed if it contains a MyChild instance. In some situations this may not be known until run-time. When this is the case dynamic cast is a better choice than static cast.

```
// Succeeds for a MyChild object
MyChild *child = dynamic_cast<MyChild*>(base);
```

If the base-to-derived conversion had been performed using a static cast instead of a dynamic cast the conversion would not have failed. It would have returned a pointer that referred to an incomplete object. Dereferencing such a pointer can lead to run-time errors.

```
// Allowed, but invalid
MyChild *child = static_cast<MyChild*>(base);
```

```
// Incomplete MyChild object dereferenced
(*child);
```

CHAPTER 27

Templates

Templates provide a way to make a class, function, or variable operate with different data types without having to rewrite the code for each type.

Function Templates

The example below shows a function that swaps two integer arguments.

```
void swap(int& a, int& b)
{
  int tmp = a;
  a = b;
  b = tmp;
}
```

To convert this method into a function template that can work with any type the first step is to add a *template parameter declaration* before the function. This declaration includes the template keyword followed by the keyword class and the name of the *template parameter*, both enclosed between angle brackets. The name of the template parameter may be anything, but it is common to name it with a capital T.

```
template<class T>
```

Alternatively, the keyword typename can be used instead of class. They are both equivalent in this context.

```
template<typename T>
```

The second step in creating a function template is to replace the data type that will be made generic with the template parameter.

```
template<class T>
void swap(T& a, T& b)
{
  T tmp = a;
  a = b;
  b = tmp;
}
```

Calling Function Templates

The function template is now complete. To use it swap can be called as if it was a regular function, but with the desired template argument specified in angle brackets before the function arguments. Behind the scenes, the compiler will instantiate a new function with this template parameter filled in, and it is this generated function that will be called from this line.

```
int a = 1, b = 2;
swap<int>(a,b); // calls int version of swap
```

Every time the function template is called with a new type, the compiler will instantiate another function using the template.

```
bool c = true, d = false;
swap<bool>(c,d); // calls bool version of swap
```

In this example, the swap function template may also be called without specifying the template parameter. This is because the compiler can automatically determine the type, because the function template's arguments use the template type. However, if this is not the case, or if there is a need to force the compiler to select a specific instantiation of the function template, the template parameter would then need to be explicitly specified within angle brackets.

```
int e = 1, f = 2;
swap(e,f); // calls int version of swap
```

Multiple Template Parameters

Templates can be defined to accept more than one template parameter by adding them between the angle brackets.

```
template<class T, class U>
void swap(T& a, U& b)
{
  T tmp = a;
  a = b;
  b = tmp;
}
```

The second template parameter in the example above allows swap to be called with two arguments of different types.

```
int main()
{
  int a = 1;
  long b = 2;
  swap<int, long>(a,b);
}
```

Class Templates

Class templates allow class members to use template parameters as types. They are created in the same way as function templates.

```
template<class T>
class myBox
{
 public:
  T a, b;
};
```

Unlike function templates, a class template must always be instantiated with explicitly specified template parameters.

```
myBox<int> box;
```

Another thing to remember when using class templates is that if a method is defined outside of the class template that definition must also be preceded by the template declaration.

```
template<class T>
class myBox
{
 public:
  T a, b;
  void swap();
};

template<class T>
void myBox<T>::swap()
{
  T tmp = a;
  a = b;
  b = tmp;
}
```

Notice that the template parameter is included in the swap template function definition after the class name qualifier. This specifies that the function's template parameter is the same as the template parameter of the class.

Non-Type Parameters

In addition to type parameters, templates can also have regular function-like parameters. As an example, the int template parameter below is used to specify the size of an array.

```
template<class T, int N>
class myBox
{
 public:
  T store[N];
};
```

When this class template is instantiated, both a type and an integer have to be included.

```
myBox<int, 5> box;
```

Default Types and Values

Class template parameters can be given default values and types.

```
template<class T = int, int N = 5>
```

To use these defaults the angle brackets just need to be left empty when instantiating the class template.

```
myBox<> box;
```

Note that default template parameters may not be used in function templates.

Class Template Specialization

If there is a need to define a different implementation for a template when a specific type is passed as the template parameter, a *template specialization* can be declared. For example, in the following class template there is a print method that outputs the value of a template variable.

```
#include <iostream>

template<class T>
class myBox
{
 public:
  T a;
  void print() { std::cout << a; }
};
```

When the template parameter is a bool the method should print out "true" or "false" instead of "1" or "0". One way to do this would be to create a *class template specialization*. A reimplementation of the class template is then created where the template parameter list is empty. Instead, a bool specialization parameter is placed after the class template's name and this data type is used instead of the template parameter throughout the implementation.

```
template<>
class myBox<bool>
{
 public:
  bool a;
  void print() { std::cout << (a ? "true" : "false"); }
};
```

When this class template is instantiated with a bool template type, this template specialization will be used instead of the standard one.

```
int main()
{
  myBox<bool> box = { true };
  box.print(); // "true"
}
```

Note that there is no inheritance of members from the standard template to the specialized template. The whole class will have to be redefined.

Function Template Specialization

Since there is only one function that is different between the templates in the example above, a better alternative would be to create a *function template specialization*. This kind of specialization looks very similar to the class template specialization, but is only applied to a single function instead of the whole class.

```
#include <iostream>

template<class T>
class myBox
{
 public:
  T a;

  template<class T> void print() {
    std::cout << a;
  }

  template<> void print<bool>() {
    std::cout << (a ? "true" : "false");
  }
};
```

This way only the print method has to be redefined and not the whole class.

```
int main()
{
  myBox<bool> box = { true };
  box.print<bool>(); // "true"
}
```

Notice that the template parameter has to be specified when the specialized function is invoked. This is not the case with the class template specialization.

Variable Templates

In addition to function and class templates, C++14 allows variables to be templated. This is achieved using the regular template syntax.

```
template<class T>
constexpr T pi = T(3.1415926535897932384626433L);
```

Together with the constexpr specifier, this template allows the value of the variable to be computed at compile time for a given type, without having to type cast the value.

```
int i = pi<int>;     // 3
float f = pi<float>; // 3.14...
```

Variadic Templates

C++11 allows template definitions to take a variable number of type arguments. This feature can be used as a replacement for variadic functions. To illustrate, consider the following variadic function, which returns the sum of any number of ints passed to it.

```
#include <iostream>
#include <initializer_list>
using namespace std;

int sum(initializer_list<int> numbers)
{
  int total = 0;
  for(auto& i : numbers) { total += i; }
  return total;
}
```

The initializer_list type indicates that the function accepts a brace-enclosed list as its argument, so the function must be called in this manner.

```
int main()
{
  cout << sum( { 1, 2, 3 } ); // "6"
}
```

The next example changes this function into a variadic template function. Such a function is traversed recursively rather than iteratively, so once the first argument has been handled the function calls itself with the remaining arguments.

The variadic template parameter is specified using the ellipsis (...) operator, followed by a name. This defines a so-called parameter pack. The parameter pack is here bound to a parameter in the function (... rest), and then unpacked into separate arguments (rest ...) when the function calls itself recursively.

```
int sum() { return 0; } // end condition

template<class T0, class ... Ts>
decltype(auto) sum(T0 first, Ts ... rest)
{
  return first + sum(rest ...);
}
```

This variadic template function can be called as a regular function, with any number of arguments. In contrast to the previously defined variadic function, this template function accepts arguments of any type.

```
int main()
{
  cout << sum(1, 1.5, true); // "3.5"
}
```

CHAPTER 28

Headers

When a project grows it is common to split the code up into different source files. When this happens the interface and implementation are generally separated. The interface is placed in a header file, which commonly has the same name as the source file and a .h file extension. This header file contains forward declarations for the source file entities that need to be accessible to other compilation units in the project. A compilation unit consists of a source file (.cpp) plus any included header files (.h or .hpp).

Why to Use Headers

C++ requires everything to be declared before it can be used. It is not enough to simply compile the source files in the same project. For example, if a function is placed in MyFunc.cpp, and a second file named MyApp.cpp in the same project tries to call it, the compiler will report that it cannot find the function.

```
// MyFunc.cpp
void myFunc() {}

// MyApp.cpp
int main()
{
  myFunc(); // error: myFunc identifier not found
}
```

To make this work the function's prototype has to be included in MyApp.cpp.

```
// MyApp.cpp
void myFunc(); // prototype

int main()
{
  myFunc();    // ok
}
```

Using Headers

This can be made more convenient if the prototype is placed in a header file named MyFunc.h and this header is included in MyApp.cpp through the use of the #include directive. This way if any changes are made to MyFunc there is no need to update the prototypes in MyApp.cpp. Furthermore, any source file that wants to use the shared code in MyFunc can just include this one header.

```
// MyFunc.h
void myFunc(); // prototype

// MyApp.cpp
#include "MyFunc.h"
```

What to Include in Headers

As far as the compiler is concerned there is no difference between a header file and a source file. The distinction is only conceptual. The key idea is that the header should contain the interface of the implementation file – that is, the code that other source files will need to use. This may include shared constants, macros, and type aliases.

```
// MyApp.h - Interface
#define DEBUG 0
const double E = 2.72;
typedef unsigned long ulong;
```

As already mentioned, the header can contain prototypes of the shared functions defined in the source file.

```
void myFunc(); // prototype
```

Additionally, shared classes are typically specified in the header, while their methods are implemented in the source file.

```
// MyApp.h class MyClass
{
  public:
    void myMethod();
};

// MyApp.cpp
void MyClass::myMethod() {}
```

As with functions, it is necessary to forward declare global variables before they can be referenced in a compilation unit outside the one containing their definition. This is done by placing the shared variable in the header and marking it with the keyword extern. This keyword indicates that the variable is initialized in another compilation unit. Functions are extern by default, so function prototypes do not need to include this specifier. Keep in mind that global variables and functions may be declared externally multiple times in a program, but they may be defined only once.

```
// MyApp.h
extern int myGlobal;
```

```
// MyApp.cpp
int myGlobal = 0;
```

It should be noted that the use of shared global variables is discouraged. This is because the larger a program becomes, the more difficult it is to keep track of which functions access and modify these variables. The preferred method is to instead pass variables to functions only as needed, in order to minimize the scope of those variables.

The header should not include any executable statements, with two exceptions. First, if a shared class method or global function is declared as `inline`, that function must be defined in the header. Otherwise, calling the inline function from another source file will give an unresolved external error. Note that the inline modifier suppresses the single definition rule that normally applies to code entities.

```
// MyApp.h
inline void inlineFunc() {}

class MyClass
{
  public:
        void inlineMethod() {}
};
```

The second exception is shared templates. When encountering a template instantiation, the compiler needs to have access to the implementation of that template, in order to create an instance of it with the type arguments filled in. The declaration and implementation of templates are therefore generally put into the header file all together.

```
// MyApp.h
template<class T>
class MyTemp { /* ... */ }
```

```
// MyApp.cpp
MyTemp<int> o;
```

Instantiating a template with the same type in many compilation units leads to significant redundant work done by the compiler and linker. To prevent this C++11 introduced extern template declarations. A template instantiation marked as extern signals to the compiler not to instantiate the template in this compilation unit.

```
// MyApp.cpp
MyTemp<int> b; // instantiation is done here

// MyFunc.cpp
extern MyTemp<int> a; // supress redundant instantiation
```

If a header requires other headers it is common to include those files as well, to make the header stand alone. This ensures that everything needed is included in the correct order, solving potential dependency problems for every source file that requires the header.

```
// MyApp.h
#include <cstddef.h> // include size_t
void mySize(std::size_t);
```

Note that since headers mainly contain declarations, any extra headers included should not affect the size of the program, although they may slow down compilation.

Include Guards

An important thing to bear in mind when using header files is that a shared code entity may only be defined once. Consequently, including the same header file more than once will likely result in compilation errors. The standard way to prevent this is to use a so-called *include guard*. An include guard is created by enclosing the start of the header in a #ifndef section that checks for a macro specific to that header file. Only when the macro is not defined is the file included and the macro is then defined, which effectively prevents the file from being included again.

```
// MyApp.h
#ifndef MYAPP_H
#define MYAPP_H
// ...
#endif // MYAPP_H
```

Index

Get the eBook for only $5!

Why limit yourself?

Now you can take the weightless companion with you wherever you go and access your content on your PC, phone, tablet, or reader.

Since you've purchased this print book, we're happy to offer you the eBook in all 3 formats for just $5.

Convenient and fully searchable, the PDF version enables you to easily find and copy code—or perform examples by quickly toggling between instructions and applications. The MOBI format is ideal for your Kindle, while the ePUB can be utilized on a variety of mobile devices.

To learn more, go to www.apress.com/companion or contact support@apress.com.

Apress®
THE EXPERT'S VOICE™

Printed in the United States
By Bookmasters